LET'S PLAY WITH EXCEL

51 ORIGINAL & USEFUL MACROS

ANURAG S PANDEY

Made with ♥ on the Notion Press Platform
www.notionpress.com

Contents

Contents

Preface

Dear Reader! I am Anurag Pandey. I am a writer, a poet and also a passionate programmer. I like writing codes. I used coding to automate required tasks in my office, which have reduced particular tasks completion time from hours and even days to just a few minutes. I remember, once an official from Income Tax Department of India had said to me that you are an Excel expert. I had replied him that I am not an Excel expert. I only use logic in anything, if I can.

We know that Excel is a very powerful application. But we only use it for simple data entry purpose. We do some plus-minus and a little multiplication etc. and all that. Let's do little more with Excel. Let's play with excel.

"Let's Play with Excel" has 51 Macros written by me. They are useful programs having original VBA coding. If you are Computer Student/ VBA Learner/ Excel Professional then you would find this book really helpful. I would like to tell you about a few programs of this book here.

One of its' Macro is able to give you ready to print Invoice with auto retrieving data. Another Macro is able to take details of entire class (any number of students and subjects) and to provide ready to print Mark-sheet of each student along with Result Sheet of all students at one place.

Another Macro provides you simple and easy format to enter data of one or many Invoice/s at once. Then another Macro creates JSON file from that data, which you can use for bulk upload for generating E Invoices.

Other two Macros are able to Encode/Decode data of your Excel sheet. Using this you can encode your data and can send the encoded Excel file on Mails etc. At the other hand the file can be decoded only if you have provided the Macro for decoding the sheet. You can very easily make changes in those Macros and then you would have unique Macros for encoding and decoding your Excel sheets.

Another Macro of this book has the ability to check two sheets and to list all those cells which have dissimilar data along with both the data. Using this you can check for changes in two sheets having similar data with some expected/ unexpected/ accidental/ unknown mismatches.

Some Macros from this book would help you to learn and do manipulation of data your way, some other would help you to exercise logic and programming and some other would help you to learn a little about

Excel and VBA.

With great excitement and expectation, I request you to check "Let's Play with Excel" and provide your invaluable feedback.

ANURAG S PANDEY

Bhubaneshwar, India

Important Instruction

Create a Macro Enabled Workbook; name it “Play with Excel.xlsm” with at least one Sheet named “Sheet1”. Get the Code starting below to the end of this book to the Visual Basic Editor of that Workbook. And now you are ready to play with excel. All the best!

1

Simple If Statement

Sub Ex01_Simple_If_Statement()

'We shall prompt the user to enter an alphabet and will reply him/her whether it was Vowel or Consonant.

```
Dim s As String
s = InputBox("Please enter an Alphabet.")
s = Left(s, 1)
s = UCase(s)
If s = "A" Or s = "E" Or s = "I" Or s = "O" Or s = "U" Then
MsgBox ("You had entered a Vowel.")
ElseIf Asc(s) > 64 And Asc(s) < 91 Then
MsgBox ("You had entered a Consonant.")
Else
MsgBox ("You had not entered a Alphabet.")
End If
End Sub
```

2

Simple If Statement Example 2

Sub Ex02_Simple_If_Statement()

```
'We shall prompt the user to enter a Digit. Then we shall tell the user whether it was Odd or Even.
    Dim i As String
    i = InputBox("Enter a digit.")
    If IsNumeric(i) = True Then
    If Int(i) <> i Then
    MsgBox ("You didn’t enter an Integer. So we shall convert it in to an Integer i.e. from " & i & " to " & Int(i) & " .")
    i = Int(i)
    End If
    If i Mod 2 = 0 Then
    MsgBox ("You had entered " & i & ". It is an Even number.")
    Else
    MsgBox ("You had entered " & i & ". It is an Odd number.")
    End If
    Else
    MsgBox ("You hadn’t entered a Digit!")
    End If
    End Sub
```

3

Nested_If

Sub Ex03_Nested_If()

```
'Logic - Any Male >= 18 Years, citizen of India, having Income >= 50000 per month, having Cricket as hobby can participate in the game.
    Dim s, s1 As String
    Dim i As Long
    s = InputBox("Enter your name.")
    s = UCase(s)
    i = 0
    While i < 1 Or i > 100
    s1 = InputBox("Hello " & s & "!" & Chr(10) & "Please enter your age in years.")
    If IsNumeric(s1) = True Then i = s1
    Wend
    If i >= 18 Then
    s1 = InputBox(s & "! Please enter your Country of Citizenship.")
    s1 = UCase(s1)
    If s1 = "INDIA" Then
    i = 0
    While i < 1 Or i > 100000000
    s1 = InputBox(s & "! Please enter your Monthly Income.")
    If IsNumeric(s1) = True Then i = s1
    Wend
    If i >= 50000 Then
    s1 = InputBox("Enter you Hobby, please.")
```

```
s1 = UCase(s1)
If s1 = "CRICKET" Then
MsgBox ("Congrats " & s & "! you can participate in this Game!")
Else
MsgBox ("Sorry " & s & "! Due to your Hobby mismatch, you can’t participate in this Game!")
End If
Else
MsgBox ("Sorry " & s & "! Due to your Income mismatch, you can’t participate in this Game!")
End If
Else
MsgBox ("Sorry " & s & "! Due to your Country of Citizenship mismatch, you can’t participate in this Game!")
End If
Else
MsgBox ("Sorry " & s & "! Due to your Age mismatch, you can’t participate in this Game!")
End If
End Sub
```

4

Nested If Elseif

Sub Ex04_Nested_If_Elseif()

'We shall ask the user to give answers of 5 questtions. Then we shall provide performance level. Zero correct answer - performance Very Poor, one - Poor, two - Satisfactory, three - Good, Four - Very Good, Five - Excellent.

```
    Dim s As String
    Dim j As Integer
    s = ""
    i = 0
    s = InputBox("What is Square Root of 100?")
    If IsNumeric(s) = True Then
    If Int(s) = 10 Then j = j + 1
    End If
    s = InputBox(" 100 + 20 * 15 / 2 + 14 / 2 * 2 = ???")
    If IsNumeric(s) = True Then
    If Int(s) = 264 Then j = j + 1
    End If
    s = InputBox(" 100 + ( 20 * 15 / 2 + 14) / 2 * 2 = ???")
    If IsNumeric(s) = True Then
    If Int(s) = 264 Then j = j + 1
    End If
    s = InputBox(" 100 + 20 * ( 15 / 2 + 14 / 2 ) * 2 = ???")
    If IsNumeric(s) = True Then
    If Int(s) = 680 Then j = j + 1
    End If
```

```
s = InputBox(" 100 + 20 * 15 / ( 2 + 14 / 2 * 2 ) + 0.25 = ???")
If IsNumeric(s) = True Then
If Int(s) = 119 Then j = j + 1
End If
If j = 0 Then
MsgBox ("You scored " & j & " out of 5. Your performance level is Very Poor!")
ElseIf j = 1 Then
MsgBox ("You scored " & j & " out of 5. Your performance level is Poor!")
ElseIf j = 2 Then
MsgBox ("You scored " & j & " out of 5. Your performance level is Satisfactory!")
ElseIf j = 3 Then
MsgBox ("You scored " & j & " out of 5. Your performance level is Good!")
ElseIf j = 4 Then
MsgBox ("You scored " & j & " out of 5. Your performance level is Very Good!")
Else
MsgBox ("You scored " & j & " out of 5. Your performance level is Excellent!")
End If
End Sub
```

5

For Next Loop

Sub Ex05_For_Next_Loop()

'We shall fill ActiveSheet Cells A2 to A11, B2 to B11... J2 to J11 with sum of previous numbers starting from 1.

'So we need a loop to run the code 100 times. And after each 10 we need to change the column.

```
Dim i, j, rows, cols As Integer
rows = 2
cols = 1
For i = 1 To 100
j = j + i
Cells(rows, cols).Value = j
If i Mod 10 = 0 Then
cols = cols + 1
rows = 2
Else
rows = rows + 1
End If
Next
End Sub
```

6

For Next Nested Loop

Sub Ex06_For_Next_Nested_Loop()

```
'We shall fill ActiveSheet Cells A2 to A11, B2 to B11... J2 to J11 with sum of previous numbers starting from 1.
    'We shall run a nested loop of 10 * 10.
    Dim i, j, k As Integer
    k = 0
    For i = 1 To 10
    For j = 1 To 10
    k = k + (i - 1) * 10 + j
    Cells(j + 1, i).Value = k
    Next
    Next
    End Sub
```

7

Print Invoice with Retrieving Data

Sub Print_Invoice_with_Retrieving_Data()

'This Macro prepares format, formulas and design of Ready-to-Print Invoice in the ActiveSheet. This Macro also prepares Column U for entry of Invoice Data in Column V to Column AE. As and when Data is entered in cells in Column V to AE, it automatically gets entered in the Invoice. Next time when you Run this Macro, it doesn't delete data of Column V to Column AE , so you don't need to re-enter unchanging data again (like Seller & Buyer details, Items details, Bank details etc.)

```
    Dim I As Integer
    ActiveSheet.Range("A1:T1").EntireColumn.Delete
    ActiveSheet.Range("A1:T1").EntireColumn.Insert
    ActiveSheet.Range("V1:V5, V8:V09, V11:V12, V15:V17, V19:V27, V29:V40").NumberFormat = "General"
    ActiveSheet.Range("V6:V7, V10, V13, V28, V42:W64, Y42:Y53").NumberFormat = "@"
    ActiveSheet.Range("V14, V18").NumberFormat = "dd/mm/yyyy"
    ActiveSheet.Range("Z42:Z53").Select
    Selection.NumberFormat = "0.00"
    Range("AB42:AD53").Select
    Selection.NumberFormat = "0.0"
    ActiveSheet.Range("U1").VALUE = "Particulars"
    ActiveSheet.Range("V1").VALUE = "Values"
```

```
ActiveSheet.Range("U2").VALUE = "Subject to XXX jurisdiction"
ActiveSheet.Range("U3").VALUE = "Your Company Name"
ActiveSheet.Range("U4").VALUE = "Your Company Address Line 1"
ActiveSheet.Range("U5").VALUE = "Address Line 2"
ActiveSheet.Range("U6").VALUE = "PHONE NO."
ActiveSheet.Range("U7").VALUE = "FSSAI NO."
ActiveSheet.Range("U8").VALUE = "PAN"
ActiveSheet.Range("U9").VALUE = "GSTIN"
ActiveSheet.Range("U10").VALUE = "TAN"
ActiveSheet.Range("U11").VALUE = "EMAIL"
ActiveSheet.Range("U12").VALUE = "IRN:"
ActiveSheet.Range("U13").VALUE = "ACK. NO."
ActiveSheet.Range("U14").VALUE = "ACK. DATE"
ActiveSheet.Range("U15").VALUE = "CASH/CREDIT"
ActiveSheet.Range("U16").VALUE = "BILL OF SUPPLY OR TAX INVOICE"
ActiveSheet.Range("U17").VALUE = "Invoice No."
ActiveSheet.Range("U18").VALUE = "Invoice Date"
ActiveSheet.Range("U19").VALUE = "State"
ActiveSheet.Range("U20").VALUE = "State Code"
ActiveSheet.Range("U21").VALUE = "Veh. No."
ActiveSheet.Range("U22").VALUE = "Owner"
ActiveSheet.Range("U23").VALUE = "Driver"
ActiveSheet.Range("U24").VALUE = "DL No."
ActiveSheet.Range("U25").VALUE = "Owner's PAN"
ActiveSheet.Range("U26").VALUE = "Transporter"
ActiveSheet.Range("U27").VALUE = "Transporter GST"
ActiveSheet.Range("U28").VALUE = "Transporter PH"
ActiveSheet.Range("U29").VALUE = "BILL TO PARTY Name"
ActiveSheet.Range("U30").VALUE = "BILL TO PARTY Address"
ActiveSheet.Range("U31").VALUE = "BILL TO PARTY Place"
ActiveSheet.Range("U32").VALUE = "BILL TO PARTY GSTIN"
ActiveSheet.Range("U33").VALUE = "BILL TO PARTY State"
ActiveSheet.Range("U34").VALUE = "BILL TO PARTY State Code"
ActiveSheet.Range("U35").VALUE = "DELIVER TO PARTY Name"
ActiveSheet.Range("U36").VALUE = "DELIVER TO PARTY Address"
ActiveSheet.Range("U37").VALUE = "DELIVER TO PARTY Place"
ActiveSheet.Range("U38").VALUE = "DELIVER TO PARTY GSTIN"
ActiveSheet.Range("U39").VALUE = "DELIVER TO PARTY State"
```

```
ActiveSheet.Range("U40").VALUE = "DELIVER TO PARTY State Code"
ActiveSheet.Range("U41").VALUE = "SL NO."
ActiveSheet.Range("V41").VALUE = "Product Description"
ActiveSheet.Range("W41").VALUE = "HSN"
ActiveSheet.Range("X41").VALUE = "Qty."
ActiveSheet.Range("Y41").VALUE = "Unit"
ActiveSheet.Range("Z41").VALUE = "Unit Price"
ActiveSheet.Range("AA41").VALUE = "Free Unit"
ActiveSheet.Range("AB41").VALUE = "IGST %"
ActiveSheet.Range("AC41").VALUE = "CGST %"
ActiveSheet.Range("AD41").VALUE = "SGST %"
ActiveSheet.Range("AE41").VALUE = "Other Charges"
ActiveSheet.Range("U1").ColumnWidth = 30
ActiveSheet.Range("V1").ColumnWidth = 20
ActiveSheet.Range("W1:AE1").ColumnWidth = 10
For I = 1 To 12
ActiveSheet.Range("U" & I + 41).VALUE = I
Next
ActiveSheet.Range("U57").VALUE = "Your Bank Details"
ActiveSheet.Range("U58").VALUE = "Bank Name"
ActiveSheet.Range("U59").VALUE = "IFSC Code"
ActiveSheet.Range("U60").VALUE = "A/c No."
ActiveSheet.Range("U61").VALUE = "Bank's Branch"
ActiveSheet.Range("U62").VALUE = "Currency Name"
ActiveSheet.Range("U63").VALUE = "Currency Short Name"
ActiveSheet.Range("U64").VALUE = "Currency Symbol"
ActiveSheet.Range("U1:AE64").Select
With Selection
.HorizontalAlignment = xlLeft
.VerticalAlignment = xlCenter
.WrapText = False
End With
With Selection.Font
.Name = "Arial Unicode MS"
.Size = 10
.Strikethrough = False
.Superscript = False
.Subscript = False
```

```
.OutlineFont = False
.Shadow = False
.Underline = xlUnderlineStyleNone
.ThemeColor = xlThemeColorLight1
.TintAndShade = 0
.ThemeFont = xlThemeFontNone
End With
'SETTING COLUMNS WIDTH AND ROWS HEIGHT
Range("A1").ColumnWidth = 0.58
Range("B1").ColumnWidth = 2.29
Range("C1").ColumnWidth = 14
Range("D1, S1").ColumnWidth = 5
Range("E1, F1").ColumnWidth = 4
Range("G1").ColumnWidth = 6.43
Range("H1").ColumnWidth = 4.14
Range("I1").ColumnWidth = 6.75
Range("J1").ColumnWidth = 8.43
Range("K1, M1, O1, Q1").ColumnWidth = 2.57
Range("L1, N1, P1, R1").ColumnWidth = 6
Range("T1").ColumnWidth = 8.86
Range("A1").RowHeight = 11.25
Range("A2, A17, A36, A41, A43:A47, A49:A50").RowHeight = 15
Range("A3").RowHeight = 22.25
Range("A4, A5, A16, A37:A40").RowHeight = 17.25
Range("A6:A7, A9, A11:A15, A18").RowHeight = 16.5
Range("A8").RowHeight = 23.5
Range("A10").RowHeight = 14.25
Range("A19:A22").RowHeight = 15
Range("A23").RowHeight = 40.5
Range("A24:A35").RowHeight = 30
Range("A42").RowHeight = 18.75
Range("A48").RowHeight = 7.5
'SETTING PAGE SETUP
With ActiveSheet.PageSetup
.LeftMargin = Application.InchesToPoints(0.2)
.RightMargin = Application.InchesToPoints(0)
.TopMargin = Application.InchesToPoints(0.25)
.BottomMargin = Application.InchesToPoints(0)
```

```
.HeaderMargin = Application.InchesToPoints(0.3)
.FooterMargin = Application.InchesToPoints(0.3)
.PrintHeadings = False
.PrintGridlines = False
.PrintComments = xlPrintNoComments
.PrintQuality = 600
.CenterHorizontally = False
.CenterVertically = False
.Orientation = xlPortrait
.Draft = False
.PaperSize = xlPaperA4
.FirstPageNumber = xlAutomatic
.Order = xlDownThenOver
.BlackAndWhite = False
.Zoom = 85
.PrintErrors = xlPrintErrorsDisplayed
.ScaleWithDocHeaderFooter = True
.AlignMarginsHeaderFooter = True
End With
'DOING FORMATTING
Range("A1:T50").Select
With Selection
.HorizontalAlignment = xlCenter
.VerticalAlignment = xlCenter
.WrapText = False
End With
With Selection.Font
.Name = "Arial Unicode MS"
.Size = 12
.Strikethrough = False
.Superscript = False
.Subscript = False
.OutlineFont = False
.Shadow = False
.Underline = xlUnderlineStyleNone
.ThemeColor = xlThemeColorLight1
.TintAndShade = 0
.ThemeFont = xlThemeFontNone
```

```
End With
Range("B23:T23, C24:C35, F24:F35, D18:J19, N18:T19, B38:I39, L41:T42").Select
With Selection
.WrapText = True
End With
Range("B2:T2, B3:T3, B4:T4, B5:T5, B6:C6, D6:F6, G6:I6, J6:L6, M6:P6, Q6:T6, B7:C7, D7:F7, G7:I7, J7:L7, M7:P7, Q7:T7, B8:C8, D8:T8, B9:C9, D9:J9, K9:M9, N9:P9, B10:T10").Merge
Range("B11:T11, B12:C12, D12:G12, H12:I12, J12:M12, N12:Q12, R12:T12, B13:C13, D13:G13, H13:I13, J13:M13, N13:Q13, R13:T13, B14:C14, D14:G14, H14:I14, J14:M14, N14:Q14, R14:T14").Merge
Range("B15:C15, D15:G15, H15:I15, J15:M15, N15:Q15, R15:T15, B16:H16, J16:T16, B17:C17, D17:J17, K17:M17, N17:T17, B18:C18, D18:J19, K18:M18, N18:T19, B20:C20, D20:J20, K20:M20, N20:T20").Merge
Range("B21:C21, D21:J21, K21:M21, N21:T21, B22:C22, D22:G22, H22:I22, K22:M22, N22:Q22, R22:S22, K36:L36, M36:N36, O36:P36, Q36:R36").Merge
Range("B37:C37, J37:O37, P37:T37, B38:I39, J38:O38, P38:T38, J39:O39, P39:T39, B40:C40, D40:I40, J40:O40, P40:T40, L41:T42, B46:D46, L46:T46, B47:E47, F47:I47, J47:O47, P47:T47, B49:T49").Merge
Range("Q7:T7").Select
With Selection.Font
.Size = 8
End With
Range("B2:T2, B6:T7, D18:J19, N18:T19, P37:P40, B46:T47").Select
With Selection.Font
.Size = 10
End With
Range("B46, L46").Select
With Selection
.VerticalAlignment = xlTop
End With
ActiveSheet.Range("B2").Formula = "=LEFT(U2,11) & V2 & RIGHT(U2,13)"
Range("B16, J16, D17, N17, B23:T23, D36:T36, D40, P37:P40, B38, L41, B46, L46, B49").Select
Selection.Font.Bold = True
Range("B3:T3").Select
Selection.Font.Bold = True
```

```
With Selection.Font
.Size = 16
End With
ActiveSheet.Range("B3").Formula = "=V3"
Range("B16:T16").Select
With Selection.Font
.Size = 13
End With
Range("B23:T23").Select
With Selection.Font
.Size = 7.5
End With
Range("B4:T4").Select
ActiveSheet.Range("B4").Formula = "=V4"
Range("B5:T5").Select
ActiveSheet.Range("B5").Formula = "=V5"
Range("B8:T15, B17:B22, D17, D20:D22, K17:K22, N17, N20:N22, B37:O40, L41").Select
With Selection.Font
.Size = 11
End With
Range("B38:I39").Select
With Selection.Font
.Size = 10
End With
Range("B24:T36").Select
With Selection.Font
.Size = 7
End With
Range("B6:T7").Select
With Selection
.VerticalAlignment = xlTop
End With
ActiveSheet.Range("B6").VALUE = "PHONE NO."
ActiveSheet.Range("B7").Formula = "=V6"
ActiveSheet.Range("D6").VALUE = "FSSAI NO."
ActiveSheet.Range("D7").Formula = "=V7"
ActiveSheet.Range("G6").VALUE = "PAN"
```

```
ActiveSheet.Range("G7").Formula = "=V8"
ActiveSheet.Range("J6").VALUE = "GSTIN"
ActiveSheet.Range("J7").Formula = "=V9"
ActiveSheet.Range("M6").VALUE = "TAN"
ActiveSheet.Range("M7").Formula = "=V10"
ActiveSheet.Range("Q6").VALUE = "EMAIL"
ActiveSheet.Range("Q7").Formula = "=V11"
Range("B8:T9, B12:T15, B17:T22, C24:C35, B37, B40, J37:J40, B47:T47").Select
With Selection
.HorizontalAlignment = xlLeft
End With
Range("B8:T8").Select
With Selection
.VerticalAlignment = xlBottom
End With
Range("B8").VALUE = "IRN:"
ActiveSheet.Range("D8").Formula = "=V12"
Range("B9").VALUE = "ACK. NO."
ActiveSheet.Range("D9").Formula = "=V13"
Range("K9").VALUE = "ACK. DATE"
ActiveSheet.Range("N9").Formula = "=V14"
Range("B10").Formula = "=V15"
Range("B11").Formula = "=V16"
Range("B11:C11").Select
Selection.Font.Bold = True
Range("B12").VALUE = "Invoice No."
ActiveSheet.Range("D12").Formula = "=V17"
Range("H12").VALUE = "Veh No."
ActiveSheet.Range("J12").Formula = "=V21"
Range("N12").VALUE = "Owner's PAN"
ActiveSheet.Range("R12").Formula = "=V25"
Range("B13").VALUE = "Invoice Date"
ActiveSheet.Range("D13").Formula = "=V18"
Range("H13").VALUE = "Owner"
ActiveSheet.Range("J13").Formula = "=V22"
Range("N13").VALUE = "Transporter"
ActiveSheet.Range("R13").Formula = "=V26"
Range("B14").VALUE = "State"
```

```
ActiveSheet.Range("D14").Formula = "=V19"
Range("H14").VALUE = "Driver"
ActiveSheet.Range("J14").Formula = "=V23"
Range("N14").VALUE = "Transporter GST"
ActiveSheet.Range("R14").Formula = "=V27"
Range("B15").VALUE = "State Code"
ActiveSheet.Range("D15").Formula = "=V20"
Range("H15").VALUE = "DL No."
ActiveSheet.Range("J15").Formula = "=V24"
Range("N15").VALUE = "Transporter PH"
ActiveSheet.Range("R15").Formula = "=V28"
Range("B16").VALUE = "BILL TO PARTY"
Range("J16").VALUE = "DELIVER TO PARTY"
Range("B17, K17").VALUE = "Name"
ActiveSheet.Range("D17").Formula = "=V29"
ActiveSheet.Range("N17").Formula = "=V35"
Range("B18, K18").VALUE = "Address"
ActiveSheet.Range("D18").Formula = "=V30"
ActiveSheet.Range("N18").Formula = "=V36"
Range("B20, K20").VALUE = "Place"
ActiveSheet.Range("D20").Formula = "=V31"
ActiveSheet.Range("N20").Formula = "=V37"
Range("B21, K21").VALUE = "GSTIN"
ActiveSheet.Range("D21").Formula = "=V32"
ActiveSheet.Range("N21").Formula = "=V38"
Range("B22, K22").VALUE = "State"
ActiveSheet.Range("D22").Formula = "=V33"
ActiveSheet.Range("N22").Formula = "=V39"
Range("H22, R22").VALUE = "St Code"
ActiveSheet.Range("J22").Formula = "=V34"
ActiveSheet.Range("T22").Formula = "=V40"
Range("B11:T49, B17:J22").Select
Selection.Borders(xlDiagonalDown).LineStyle = xlNone
Selection.Borders(xlDiagonalUp).LineStyle = xlNone
With Selection.Borders(xlEdgeLeft)
.LineStyle = xlContinuous
.ColorIndex = 0
.TintAndShade = 0
```

```
.Weight = xlThin
End With
With Selection.Borders(xlEdgeTop)
.LineStyle = xlContinuous
.ColorIndex = 0
.TintAndShade = 0
.Weight = xlThin
End With
With Selection.Borders(xlEdgeBottom)
.LineStyle = xlContinuous
.ColorIndex = 0
.TintAndShade = 0
.Weight = xlThin
End With
With Selection.Borders(xlEdgeRight)
.LineStyle = xlContinuous
.ColorIndex = 0
.TintAndShade = 0
.Weight = xlThin
End With
Selection.Borders(xlInsideVertical).LineStyle = xlNone
Selection.Borders(xlInsideHorizontal).LineStyle = xlNone
Range("B5:T5, B7:T7, B9:T9, B11:T11, B15:T15, B16:T16, B23:T23, B35:T35, B37:I37, R37:T37, R38:T38, R39:T39, B39:I39, B40:T40, B46:T46, B47:T47, B48:T48").Select
Selection.Borders(xlDiagonalDown).LineStyle = xlNone
Selection.Borders(xlDiagonalUp).LineStyle = xlNone
With Selection.Borders(xlEdgeBottom)
.LineStyle = xlContinuous
.ColorIndex = 0
.TintAndShade = 0
.Weight = xlThin
End With
Range("J37:O40, F47:I47, F47:I47, J47:O47").Select
Selection.Borders(xlDiagonalDown).LineStyle = xlNone
Selection.Borders(xlDiagonalUp).LineStyle = xlNone
With Selection.Borders(xlEdgeLeft)
.LineStyle = xlContinuous
```

```
.ColorIndex = 0
.TintAndShade = 0
.Weight = xlThin
End With
With Selection.Borders(xlEdgeRight)
.LineStyle = xlContinuous
.ColorIndex = 0
.TintAndShade = 0
.Weight = xlThin
End With
Range("B23:T36").Select
Selection.Borders(xlDiagonalDown).LineStyle = xlNone
Selection.Borders(xlDiagonalUp).LineStyle = xlNone
With Selection.Borders(xlEdgeLeft)
.LineStyle = xlContinuous
.ColorIndex = 0
.TintAndShade = 0
.Weight = xlThin
End With
With Selection.Borders(xlEdgeTop)
.LineStyle = xlContinuous
.ColorIndex = 0
.TintAndShade = 0
.Weight = xlThin
End With
With Selection.Borders(xlEdgeBottom)
.LineStyle = xlContinuous
.ColorIndex = 0
.TintAndShade = 0
.Weight = xlThin
End With
With Selection.Borders(xlEdgeRight)
.LineStyle = xlContinuous
.ColorIndex = 0
.TintAndShade = 0
.Weight = xlThin
End With
With Selection.Borders(xlInsideVertical)
```

```
.LineStyle = xlContinuous
.ColorIndex = 0
.TintAndShade = 0
.Weight = xlThin
End With
'SETTING ITEMS, RATE, TAX, AMOUNT DETAILS
Range("B23").VALUE = "Sl No"
Range("C23").VALUE = "Product Description"
Range("D23").VALUE = "HSN"
Range("E23").VALUE = "Qty."
Range("F23").VALUE = "Unit"
Range("G23").VALUE = "Unit Price"
Range("H23").VALUE = "Free Unit"
Range("I23").VALUE = "Disc. Amt."
Range("J23").VALUE = "Taxable Amt."
Range("K23").VALUE = "IGST%"
Range("L23").VALUE = "IGST Amt."
Range("M23").VALUE = "CGST%"
Range("N23").VALUE = "CGST Amt."
Range("O23").VALUE = "SGST%"
Range("P23").VALUE = "SGST Amt."
Range("Q23").VALUE = "GST%"
Range("R23").VALUE = "GST Amt."
Range("S23").VALUE = "Oth. Chrgs."
Range("T23").VALUE = "TOTAL Amt."
'SETTING FORMULAS TO CELLS
Cells(24, 9).Formula = "=IF(AND(B24<>"""", C24<>"""", E24<>"""", G24<>""""), G24*H24, """")"
Cells(24, 10).Formula = "=IF(AND(B24<>"""", C24<>"""", E24<>"""", G24<>""""), E24*G24-I24, """")"
Cells(24, 12).Formula = "=IF(AND(B24<>"""", C24<>"""", E24<>"""", G24<>""""), J24*K24%, """")"
Cells(24, 14).Formula = "=IF(AND(B24<>"""", C24<>"""", E24<>"""", G24<>""""), J24*M24%, """")"
Cells(24, 16).Formula = "=IF(AND(B24<>"""", C24<>"""", E24<>"""", G24<>""""), J24*O24%, """")"
Cells(24, 17).Formula = "=IF(AND(B24<>"""", C24<>"""", E24<>"""", G24<>""""), O24+M24+K24, """")"
```

```
Cells(24, 18).Formula = "=IF(AND(B24<>"""", C24<>"""", E24<>"""", G24<>""""), L24+N24+P24, """")"
Cells(24, 20).Formula = "=IF(AND(B24<>"""", C24<>"""", E24<>"""", G24<>""""), J24+R24+S24, """")"
I = 0
For I = 73 To 84
If I <> 75 And I <> 77 And I <> 79 And I <> 83 Then
Range(Chr(I) & 24).Select
Selection.AutoFill Destination:=Range(Chr(I) & 24 & ":" & Chr(I) & 35), Type:=xlFillDefault
End If
Next
Range("D36").VALUE = "TOTAL"
Range("E36").Formula = "=ROUND(SUM(E24:E35),2)"
Range("H36").Formula = "=ROUND(SUM(H24:H35),2)"
Range("I36").Formula = "=ROUND(SUM(I24:I35),2)"
Range("J36").Formula = "=ROUND(SUM(J24:J35),2)"
Range("K36").Formula = "=ROUND(SUM(L24:L35),2)"
Range("M36").Formula = "=ROUND(SUM(N24:N35),2)"
Range("O36").Formula = "=ROUND(SUM(P24:P35),2)"
Range("Q36").Formula = "=ROUND(K36,2) + ROUND(M36,2) + ROUND(O36,2)"
Range("S36").Formula = "=ROUND(SUM(S24:S35),2)"
Range("T36").Formula = "=ROUND(J36,2) + ROUND(K36,2) + ROUND(M36,2) + ROUND(O36,2) + ROUND(S36,2)"
Range("B37").VALUE = "Amount in Words"
Range("J37").VALUE = "Taxable Amt --||-- GST Amt"
Range("P37").Formula = "=ROUND(J36, 2) & "" --||-- "" & ROUND(Q36, 2)"
Range("J38").VALUE = "Other Charges"
Range("P38").Formula = "=S36"
Range("J39").VALUE = "TCS Amount @ 0.1%"
Range("P39").Formula = "=T36*0.1%"
Range("J40").VALUE = "Rounding Off"
Range("P40").Formula = "=((T36+P39) - ROUND(T36+P39,0))*-1"
Range("B40").VALUE = "Invoice Total"
If ActiveSheet.Range("V62").VALUE = "" Then ActiveSheet.Range("V62").VALUE = "US Dollar"
```

```
If ActiveSheet.Range("V63").VALUE = "" Then
ActiveSheet.Range("V63").VALUE = "USD"
If ActiveSheet.Range("V64").VALUE = "" Then
ActiveSheet.Range("V64").VALUE = "$"
Range("D40").Formula = "=V63 & "" "" & V64 & "" "" & IF(P40=0.50,
ROUNDUP(T36+P39,0), ROUND(T36+P39,0))"
ActiveSheet.Range("U65").VALUE = "For"
For I = 1 To Len(ActiveSheet.Range("B3").VALUE)
ActiveSheet.Range("U65").VALUE = ActiveSheet.Range("U65").VALUE & "_"
Next
Range("L41").Formula = "=U65 & CHAR(10) & "" "" & B3"
Range("B46").VALUE = "Party's Signature"
Range("L46").VALUE = "Authorised Signatory"
Range("B47").Formula = "=""Bank: "" & V58"
Range("F47").Formula = "=""IFSC: "" & V59"
Range("J47").Formula = "=""A/C: "" & V60"
Range("P47").Formula = "=""Branch: "" & V61"
Range("B49").VALUE = "Original Copy For Recipient"
'SETTING NUMBER OF ITEMS
For I = 42 To 53
ActiveSheet.Range("B" & I - 18).Formula = "=U" & I
ActiveSheet.Range("C" & I - 18).Formula = "=V" & I
ActiveSheet.Range("D" & I - 18).Formula = "=W" & I
ActiveSheet.Range("E" & I - 18).Formula = "=X" & I
ActiveSheet.Range("F" & I - 18).Formula = "=Y" & I
ActiveSheet.Range("G" & I - 18).Formula = "=Z" & I
ActiveSheet.Range("H" & I - 18).Formula = "=AA" & I
ActiveSheet.Range("K" & I - 18).Formula = "=AB" & I
ActiveSheet.Range("M" & I - 18).Formula = "=AC" & I
ActiveSheet.Range("O" & I - 18).Formula = "=AD" & I
ActiveSheet.Range("S" & I - 18).Formula = "=AE" & I
Next
For I = 42 To 53
If ActiveSheet.Range("V" & I).VALUE = "" Then Exit For
Next
Range("B7:T7, D8, D9, R15, D24:D35").NumberFormat = "@"
Range("N9, D13").NumberFormat = "dd/mm/yyyy"
```

```
Range("G24:G36, I24:J36, L24:L35, K36, N24:N35, M36, P24:P35, O36, R24:R35, Q36, S24:S36, T24:T36, R37:R40, D40").Select
Selection.NumberFormat = "0.00"
Range("M24:M35, O24:O35, Q24:Q35").Select
Selection.NumberFormat = "0.0"
I = I - 42
If I > 0 And I < 12 Then
ActiveSheet.Range("U" & 24 + I & ":AE35").Select
Selection.Insert Shift:=xlDown
ActiveSheet.Range("C" & 24 + I & ":C35").Select
Selection.EntireRow.Delete
ActiveSheet.Range("B" & 24 + I & ":T" & 24 + I).Select
Selection.Borders(xlDiagonalDown).LineStyle = xlNone
Selection.Borders(xlDiagonalUp).LineStyle = xlNone
With Selection.Borders(xlEdgeTop)
.LineStyle = xlContinuous
.ColorIndex = 0
.TintAndShade = 0
.Weight = xlThin
End With
For J = 1 To (12 - I) * 2 - 1
ActiveSheet.Range("C" & 24 + I + 5).Select
Selection.EntireRow.Insert
ActiveSheet.Range("U" & 24 + I + 5 & ":AE" & 24 + I + 5).Select
Selection.Delete Shift:=xlUp
Next
ActiveSheet.Range("C" & 24 + I + 5 & ":C" & 24 + I + 5 + (12 - I) * 2 - 1).RowHeight = 15
ActiveSheet.Range("C" & 24 + I + 10 + (12 - I) * 2 - 1).RowHeight = 30
ActiveSheet.Range("C" & 24 + I + 14 + (12 - I) * 2 - 1 & ":C" & 24 + I + 24 + (12 - I) * 2 - 1).RowHeight = 15
ActiveSheet.PageSetup.PrintArea = "$A$1:$T$" & 24 + I + 14 + (12 - I) * 2 - 1
Else
Range("B36:T36").Select
Selection.Borders(xlDiagonalDown).LineStyle = xlNone
Selection.Borders(xlDiagonalUp).LineStyle = xlNone
With Selection.Borders(xlEdgeTop)
.LineStyle = xlContinuous
```

```
.ColorIndex = 0
.TintAndShade = 0
.Weight = xlThin
End With
ActiveSheet.Range("A51:A60").RowHeight = 15
ActiveSheet.PageSetup.PrintArea = "$A$1:$T$50"
End If
MsgBox ("Please update Invoice details by filling data in Column V to AE. To update Amount in Words, Please Run this Macro again. Or you may Run the Macro named Amount_in_Words also.")
Dim S1(30), s(11), RS, rs1, SS, RUPEE, inputrow, outputrow As String
RUPEE = ""
RS = ""
S1(0) = "One "
S1(1) = "Two "
S1(2) = "Three "
S1(3) = "Four "
S1(4) = "Five "
S1(5) = "Six "
S1(6) = "Seven "
S1(7) = "Eight "
S1(8) = "Nine "
S1(9) = "Ten "
S1(10) = "Eleven "
S1(11) = "Twelve "
S1(12) = "Thirteen "
S1(13) = "Fourteen "
S1(14) = "Fifteen "
S1(15) = "Sixteen "
S1(16) = "Seventeen "
S1(17) = "Eighteen "
S1(18) = "Nineteen "
S1(19) = "Twenty "
S1(20) = "Thirty "
S1(21) = "Forty "
S1(22) = "Fifty "
S1(23) = "Sixty "
S1(24) = "Seventy "
```

```
S1(25) = "Eighty "
S1(26) = "Ninety "
S1(27) = "Hundred "
S1(28) = "Thousand "
S1(29) = "Lacs "
For I = 24 To 40
If ActiveSheet.Range("B" & I).VALUE = "Invoice Total" Then
SS = Right(ActiveSheet.Range("D" & I).VALUE, Len(ActiveSheet.Range("D" & I).VALUE) - (Len(ActiveSheet.Range("V63").VALUE) + Len(ActiveSheet.Range("V64").VALUE) + 2))
outputrow = "B" & I - 2
outputrow = Trim(outputrow)
Exit For
End If
Next
If SS = "" Then
inputrow = InputBox("Enter Input Cell Address of Amount in digits.")
SS = ActiveSheet.Range(inputrow).VALUE
outputrow = InputBox("Enter Output Cell Address for Amount in words.")
End If
SS = Trim(SS)
RUPEE = ""
RS = Int(SS)
If Len(RS) > 7 Then
rs1 = Left(RS, Len(RS) - 7)
RS = Right(RS, 7)
End If
If Len(rs1) > 7 Then rs1 = Right(rs1, 7)
PART2:
If Len(RS) = 7 Then
If Int(Left(RS, 1)) = 1 Then
s(0) = S1(Int(Mid(RS, 2, 1)) + 9)
ElseIf Int(Left(RS, 1)) > 1 Then
s(0) = S1(Int(Left(RS, 1)) + 17)
If Int(Mid(RS, 2, 1)) <> 0 Then s(1) = S1(Int(Mid(RS, 2, 1)) - 1)
Else
If Int(Mid(RS, 2, 1)) <> 0 Then s(1) = S1(Int(Mid(RS, 2, 1)) - 1)
End If
```

```
If s(0) <> "" Or s(1) <> "" Then s(2) = S1(29)
End If
If Len(RS) = 6 Then
If Int(Left(RS, 1)) > 0 Then
s(0) = S1(Int(Left(RS, 1)) - 1)
s(1) = S1(29)
End If
End If
If Len(RS) > 4 Then
If Int(Left(Right(RS, 5), 1)) = 1 Then
s(3) = S1(Int(Left(Right(RS, 4), 1)) + 9)
ElseIf Int(Left(Right(RS, 5), 1)) > 1 Then
s(3) = S1(Left(Right(RS, 5), 1) + 17)
If Int(Left(Right(RS, 4), 1)) <> 0 Then s(4) = S1(Int(Left(Right(RS, 4), 1)) - 1)
Else
If Int(Left(Right(RS, 4), 1)) <> 0 Then s(4) = S1(Int(Left(Right(RS, 4), 1)) - 1)
End If
If s(3) <> "" Or s(4) <> "" Then s(5) = S1(28)
End If
If Len(RS) = 4 Then
If Int(Left(RS, 1)) > 0 Then
s(0) = S1(Int(Left(RS, 1)) - 1)
s(1) = S1(28)
End If
End If
If Len(RS) > 2 Then
If Int(Left(Right(RS, 3), 1)) <> 0 Then
s(6) = S1(Int(Left(Right(RS, 3), 1)) - 1)
s(7) = S1(27)
End If
End If
If Len(RS) > 1 Then
If Int(Left(Right(RS, 2), 1)) = 1 Then
s(8) = S1(Int(Left(Right(RS, 1), 1)) + 9)
ElseIf Int(Left(Right(RS, 2), 1)) > 1 Then
s(8) = S1(Left(Right(RS, 2), 1) + 17)
If Int(Left(Right(RS, 1), 1)) <> 0 Then s(9) = S1(Int(Left(Right(RS, 1), 1)) - 1)
Else
```

```
If Int(Left(Right(RS, 1), 1)) <> 0 Then s(9) = S1(Int(Left(Right(RS, 1), 1)) - 1)
End If
End If
If Len(RS) = 1 Then
If Int(Left(RS, 1)) > 0 Then s(0) = S1(Int(Left(RS, 1)) - 1)
End If
RS = ""
RS = s(0) & s(1) & s(2) & s(3) & s(4) & s(5) & s(6) & s(7) & s(8) & s(9)
If RUPEE = "" Then
RUPEE = RS
Else
RUPEE = RS & "Crore " & RUPEE
End If
RUPEE = Trim(RUPEE)
If RUPEE <> "" Then ActiveSheet.Range(outputrow).VALUE = ActiveSheet.Range("V62").VALUE & " " & RUPEE & " Only."
For I = 0 To 9
s(I) = ""
Next I
RS = rs1
rs1 = ""
If Len(RS) > 0 Then GoTo PART2
Range("B2").Select
End Sub
```

8

Print Mark sheet and Result of Class

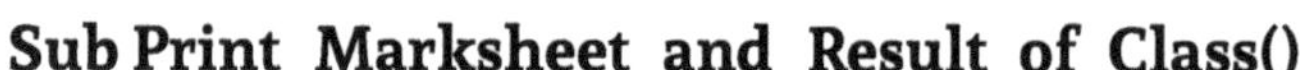

Sub Print_Marksheet_and_Result_of_Class()

```
Dim TOTSTU, TOTSUB, FRESHORPRE, FM, K, L, M As Integer
    FRESHORPRE = 0
    TOTSTU = 0
    TOTSUB = 0
    FM = 0
    ActiveSheet.Range("A6").ColumnWidth = 20
    While (FRESHORPRE < 1 Or FRESHORPRE > 2)
    s = InputBox("ENTER 1 for Fresh Start (It will delete data from the sheet), ENTER 2 for keeping previous Data.", "Class Result Program", , 600, 600)
    If IsNumeric(s) = True Then FRESHORPRE = Int(s)
    Wend
    If FRESHORPRE = 1 Then
    ActiveSheet.Range("A1:ZZ1000").Select
    Selection.EntireRow.Delete
    ActiveSheet.Range("A1").Select
    End If
    If ActiveSheet.Range("A2").Value = "" Then ActiveSheet.Range("A2").Value = UCase(InputBox("Enter Name of the Organisation.", "Class Result Program", , 600, 600))
    If ActiveSheet.Range("A3").Value = "" Then ActiveSheet.Range("A3").Value = UCase(InputBox("Enter Name of the Exam.", "Class Result Program", , 600,
```

```
600))
    If ActiveSheet.Range("A4").Value = "" Then ActiveSheet.Range("A4").Value = "Class : " & UCase(InputBox("Enter Class with Section.", "Class Result Program", , 600, 600))
    While (TOTSTU < 1)
    s = InputBox("Enter Total Number of Students in the " & ActiveSheet.Range("A4").Value, "Class Result Program", , 600, 600)
    If IsNumeric(s) = True Then TOTSTU = Int(s)
    Wend
    ActiveSheet.Range("A" & TOTSTU + 7 & ":ZZ1000").Select
    Selection.EntireRow.Delete
    If ActiveSheet.Range("A6").Value = "" Then ActiveSheet.Range("A6").Value = "Student's Name"
    ActiveSheet.Range("B6").ColumnWidth = 4.5
    If ActiveSheet.Range("B6").Value = "" Then ActiveSheet.Range("B6").Value = "Roll"
    For i = 1 To TOTSTU
    If ActiveSheet.Range("A" & i + 6).Value = "" Then ActiveSheet.Range("A" & i + 6).Value = UCase(InputBox("Enter Name of Student " & i & " .", "Class Result Program", , 600, 600))
    If ActiveSheet.Range("B" & i + 6).Value = "" Then ActiveSheet.Range("B" & i + 6).Value = InputBox("Enter Roll No. of Student " & i & " " & ActiveSheet.Range("A" & i + 6).Value & " .", "Class Result Program", , 600, 600)
    Next
    While (TOTSUB < 1)
    s = InputBox("Enter Total number of Subjects.", "Class Result Program", , 600, 600)
    If IsNumeric(s) = True Then TOTSUB = Int(s)
    Wend
    K = 2
    For i = 1 To TOTSUB * 3 Step 3
    If ActiveSheet.Range(Cells(5, i + K).Address).Value = "" Then
    ActiveSheet.Range(Cells(5, i + K).Address & ":" & Cells(5, i + K + 2).Address).Select
    Selection.Merge
    Selection.Value = UCase(InputBox("Enter Name of Subject " & Int(i / 3) + 1, "Class Result Program", , 600, 600))
```

```
ActiveSheet.Range(Cells(7, i + K).Address & ":" & Cells(1000, i + K + 2).Address).Value = ""
End If
ActiveSheet.Range(Cells(6, i + K).Address).Value = "FM"
ActiveSheet.Range(Cells(6, i + K).Address).ColumnWidth = 4
ActiveSheet.Range(Cells(6, i + K + 1).Address).Value = "Obt."
ActiveSheet.Range(Cells(6, i + K + 1).Address).ColumnWidth = 4
ActiveSheet.Range(Cells(6, i + K + 2).Address).Value = "Gr."
ActiveSheet.Range(Cells(6, i + K + 2).Address).ColumnWidth = 4
FM = 0
If IsNumeric(ActiveSheet.Range(Cells(7, i + K).Address).Value) = False Then ActiveSheet.Range(Cells(7, i + K).Address).Value = 0
If Val(ActiveSheet.Range(Cells(7, i + K).Address).Value) > 0 Then
FM = ActiveSheet.Range(Cells(7, i + K).Address).Value
Else
While (FM < 1)
s = InputBox("Enter Full Marks of " & ActiveSheet.Range(Cells(5, i + K).Address).Value & ".", "Class Result Program", , 600, 600)
If IsNumeric(s) = True Then FM = Int(s)
Wend
End If
For j = 1 To TOTSTU
ActiveSheet.Range(Cells(j + 6, i + K).Address).Value = FM
If IsNumeric(ActiveSheet.Range(Cells(j + 6, i + K + 1).Address).Value) = False Or ActiveSheet.Range(Cells(j + 6, i + K + 1).Address).Value = "" Then
REP:
s = InputBox("Enter Marks obtained by " & ActiveSheet.Range("A" & j + 6).Value & " in Subject " & ActiveSheet.Range(Cells(5, i + K).Address).Value & ".", "Class Result Program", , 600, 600)
If IsNumeric(s) = True Then
If Int(s) >= 0 And Int(s) <= FM Then
ActiveSheet.Range(Cells(j + 6, i + K + 1).Address).Value = Int(s)
Else
GoTo REP
End If
Else
GoTo REP
End If
```

```
End If
If (ActiveSheet.Range(Cells(j + 6, i + K + 1).Address).Value) / FM * 100 >=
90 Then
ActiveSheet.Range(Cells(j + 6, i + K + 2).Address).Value = "A+"
ElseIf (ActiveSheet.Range(Cells(j + 6, i + K + 1).Address).Value) / FM * 100
>= 80 Then
ActiveSheet.Range(Cells(j + 6, i + K + 2).Address).Value = "A"
ElseIf (ActiveSheet.Range(Cells(j + 6, i + K + 1).Address).Value) / FM * 100
>= 70 Then
ActiveSheet.Range(Cells(j + 6, i + K + 2).Address).Value = "B+"
ElseIf (ActiveSheet.Range(Cells(j + 6, i + K + 1).Address).Value) / FM * 100
>= 60 Then
ActiveSheet.Range(Cells(j + 6, i + K + 2).Address).Value = "B"
ElseIf (ActiveSheet.Range(Cells(j + 6, i + K + 1).Address).Value) / FM * 100
>= 50 Then
ActiveSheet.Range(Cells(j + 6, i + K + 2).Address).Value = "C+"
ElseIf (ActiveSheet.Range(Cells(j + 6, i + K + 1).Address).Value) / FM * 100
>= 40 Then
ActiveSheet.Range(Cells(j + 6, i + K + 2).Address).Value = "C"
ElseIf (ActiveSheet.Range(Cells(j + 6, i + K + 1).Address).Value) / FM * 100
>= 30 Then
ActiveSheet.Range(Cells(j + 6, i + K + 2).Address).Value = "D"
Else
ActiveSheet.Range(Cells(j + 6, i + K + 2).Address).Value = "E"
End If
Next
Next
ActiveSheet.Range("A" & j + 6 & ": zz1000").Value = ""
ActiveSheet.Range("A" & j + 6 & ": zz1000").Select
Selection.UnMerge
ActiveSheet.Range(Cells(5, i + K).Address).Value = ""
ActiveSheet.Range(Cells(5, i + K).Address & ":" & Cells(5, i + K +
2).Address).Select
Selection.UnMerge
ActiveSheet.Range(Cells(1, i + K + 1).Address & ":zz" & j + 5).Value = ""
ActiveSheet.Range(Cells(1, i + K + 1).Address & ":zz" & j + 5).Select
Selection.UnMerge
ActiveSheet.Range("A2").Select
```

```
ActiveSheet.Range(Cells(6, i + K).Address).Value = "TFM"
ActiveSheet.Range(Cells(6, i + K).Address).ColumnWidth = 5
ActiveSheet.Range(Cells(6, i + K + 1).Address).Value = "Obt."
ActiveSheet.Range(Cells(6, i + K + 1).Address).ColumnWidth = 5
ActiveSheet.Range(Cells(6, i + K + 2).Address).Value = "OA Gr."
ActiveSheet.Range(Cells(6, i + K + 2).Address).ColumnWidth = 5
ActiveSheet.Range(Cells(6, i + K + 3).Address).Value = "RANK"
ActiveSheet.Range(Cells(6, i + K + 3).Address).ColumnWidth = 5
For j = 1 To TOTSTU
FM = 0
totmarks = 0
For i = 1 To TOTSUB * 3 Step 3
FM = FM + ActiveSheet.Range(Cells(j + 6, i + K).Address).Value
totmarks = totmarks + ActiveSheet.Range(Cells(j + 6, i + K + 1).Address).Value
Next
ActiveSheet.Range(Cells(j + 6, i + K).Address).Value = FM
ActiveSheet.Range(Cells(j + 6, i + K + 1).Address).Value = totmarks
If totmarks / FM * 100 >= 90 Then
ActiveSheet.Range(Cells(j + 6, i + K + 2).Address).Value = "A+"
ElseIf totmarks / FM * 100 >= 80 Then
ActiveSheet.Range(Cells(j + 6, i + K + 2).Address).Value = "A"
ElseIf totmarks / FM * 100 >= 70 Then
ActiveSheet.Range(Cells(j + 6, i + K + 2).Address).Value = "B+"
ElseIf totmarks / FM * 100 >= 60 Then
ActiveSheet.Range(Cells(j + 6, i + K + 2).Address).Value = "B"
ElseIf totmarks / FM * 100 >= 50 Then
ActiveSheet.Range(Cells(j + 6, i + K + 2).Address).Value = "C+"
ElseIf totmarks / FM * 100 >= 40 Then
ActiveSheet.Range(Cells(j + 6, i + K + 2).Address).Value = "C"
ElseIf totmarks / FM * 100 >= 30 Then
ActiveSheet.Range(Cells(j + 6, i + K + 2).Address).Value = "D"
Else
ActiveSheet.Range(Cells(j + 6, i + K + 2).Address).Value = "E"
End If
ActiveSheet.Range(Cells(j + 6, i + K + 4).Address).Value = totmarks
ActiveSheet.Range(Cells(j + 6, i + K + 5).Address).Value = ActiveSheet.Range("B" & j + 6).Value
```

```
For jj = 1 To j
For jjj = jj + 1 To j
If ActiveSheet.Range(Cells(jj + 6, i + K + 4).Address).Value < ActiveSheet.Range(Cells(jjj + 6, i + K + 4).Address).Value Then
tmp = ActiveSheet.Range(Cells(jj + 6, i + K + 4).Address).Value
ActiveSheet.Range(Cells(jj + 6, i + K + 4).Address).Value = ActiveSheet.Range(Cells(jjj + 6, i + K + 4).Address).Value
ActiveSheet.Range(Cells(jjj + 6, i + K + 4).Address).Value = tmp
tmp = ActiveSheet.Range(Cells(jj + 6, i + K + 5).Address).Value
ActiveSheet.Range(Cells(jj + 6, i + K + 5).Address).Value = ActiveSheet.Range(Cells(jjj + 6, i + K + 5).Address).Value
ActiveSheet.Range(Cells(jjj + 6, i + K + 5).Address).Value = tmp
End If
Next
Next
Rank = 1
For jj = 2 To j
If ActiveSheet.Range(Cells(jj + 5, i + K + 4).Address).Value > ActiveSheet.Range(Cells(jj + 6, i + K + 4).Address).Value Then Rank = Rank + 1
ActiveSheet.Range(Cells(jj + 6, i + K + 6).Address).Value = Rank
Next
Next
ActiveSheet.Range(Cells(7, i + K + 6).Address).Value = 1
For jj = 1 To TOTSTU
For j = 1 To TOTSTU
If ActiveSheet.Range("B" & jj + 6).Value = ActiveSheet.Range(Cells(j + 6, i + K + 5).Address).Value Then
ActiveSheet.Range(Cells(jj + 6, i + K + 3).Address).Value = ActiveSheet.Range(Cells(j + 6, i + K + 6).Address).Value
Exit For
End If
Next
Next
s = ""
ActiveSheet.Range(Cells(6, i + K + 4).Address & ":zz" & TOTSTU + 6).Value = ""
ActiveSheet.Range("A2").Select
```

```
K = 10
For i = 1 To TOTSTU
M = K
ActiveSheet.Range("B" & TOTSTU + K & ":Q" & TOTSTU + K).Merge
ActiveSheet.Range("B" & TOTSTU + K & ":Q" & TOTSTU + K).Value =
ActiveSheet.Range("A2").Value
ActiveSheet.Range("B" & TOTSTU + K & ":Q" & TOTSTU + K).RowHeight =
25
ActiveSheet.Range("B" & TOTSTU + K & ":Q" & TOTSTU + K).Select
With Selection.Font
.Size = 20
End With
With Selection
.HorizontalAlignment = xlCenter
.VerticalAlignment = xlCenter
End With
K = K + 2
ActiveSheet.Range("B" & TOTSTU + K & ":Q" & TOTSTU + K).Merge
ActiveSheet.Range("B" & TOTSTU + K & ":Q" & TOTSTU + K).Value =
"MARKSHEET"
ActiveSheet.Range("B" & TOTSTU + K & ":Q" & TOTSTU + K).RowHeight =
20
ActiveSheet.Range("B" & TOTSTU + K & ":Q" & TOTSTU + K).Select
With Selection.Font
.Size = 17
End With
With Selection
.HorizontalAlignment = xlCenter
.VerticalAlignment = xlCenter
End With
K = K + 2
ActiveSheet.Range("B" & TOTSTU + K & ":Q" & TOTSTU + K).Merge
ActiveSheet.Range("B" & TOTSTU + K & ":Q" & TOTSTU + K).Value =
ActiveSheet.Range("A3").Value
ActiveSheet.Range("B" & TOTSTU + K + 1 & ":Q" & TOTSTU + K + 1).Merge
ActiveSheet.Range("B" & TOTSTU + K + 1 & ":Q" & TOTSTU + K + 1).Value
= ActiveSheet.Range("A4").Value
ActiveSheet.Range("B" & TOTSTU + K & ":Q" & TOTSTU + K + 1).Select
```

```
With Selection.Font
.Size = 15
End With
With Selection
.HorizontalAlignment = xlCenter
.VerticalAlignment = xlCenter
End With
K = K + 2
ActiveSheet.Range("B" & TOTSTU + K & ":I" & TOTSTU + K).Merge
ActiveSheet.Range("B" & TOTSTU + K & ":I" & TOTSTU + K).Value = "Name : " & ActiveSheet.Range("A" & i + 6).Value
ActiveSheet.Range("J" & TOTSTU + K & ":Q" & TOTSTU + K).Merge
ActiveSheet.Range("J" & TOTSTU + K & ":Q" & TOTSTU + K).Value = "Roll No. : " & ActiveSheet.Range("B" & i + 6).Value
ActiveSheet.Range("B" & TOTSTU + K & ":Q" & TOTSTU + K).Select
With Selection.Font
.Size = 13
End With
With Selection
.HorizontalAlignment = xlCenter
.VerticalAlignment = xlCenter
End With
K = K + 2
L = -1
For j = 1 To TOTSUB
L = L + 3
If L = 14 Then
L = 2
K = K + 3
End If
ActiveSheet.Range(Chr(L + 66) & TOTSTU + K & ":" & Chr(L + 68) & TOTSTU + K).Merge
ActiveSheet.Range(Chr(L + 66) & TOTSTU + K & ":" & Chr(L + 68) & TOTSTU + K).Value = ActiveSheet.Range(Cells(5, ((j - 1) * 3) + 3).Address)
ActiveSheet.Range(Chr(L + 66) & TOTSTU + K + 1 & ":" & Chr(L + 68) & TOTSTU + K + 1).Value = ActiveSheet.Range(Cells(6, ((j - 1) * 3) + 3).Address & ":" & Cells(6, ((j - 1) * 3) + 3 + 2).Address).Value
```

```
ActiveSheet.Range(Chr(L + 66) & TOTSTU + K + 2 & ":" & Chr(L + 68) & TOTSTU + K + 2).Value = ActiveSheet.Range(Cells(i + 6, ((j - 1) * 3) + 3).Address & ":" & Cells(i + 6, ((j - 1) * 3) + 3 + 2).Address).Value
ActiveSheet.Range(Chr(L + 66) & TOTSTU + K & ":" & Chr(L + 68) & TOTSTU + K + 2).Select
With Selection.Borders
.LineStyle = xlContinuous
.Weight = xlThin
End With
With Selection.Font
.Size = 11
End With
Next
K = K + 4
ActiveSheet.Range("D" & TOTSTU + K & ":F" & TOTSTU + K).Merge
ActiveSheet.Range("D" & TOTSTU + K & ":F" & TOTSTU + K).Value = "Full Marks"
ActiveSheet.Range("G" & TOTSTU + K & ":I" & TOTSTU + K).Merge
ActiveSheet.Range("G" & TOTSTU + K & ":I" & TOTSTU + K).Value = "Obtained"
ActiveSheet.Range("J" & TOTSTU + K & ":L" & TOTSTU + K).Merge
ActiveSheet.Range("J" & TOTSTU + K & ":L" & TOTSTU + K).Value = "OverAllGr."
ActiveSheet.Range("M" & TOTSTU + K & ":O" & TOTSTU + K).Merge
ActiveSheet.Range("M" & TOTSTU + K & ":O" & TOTSTU + K).Value = "Rank"
K = K + 1
j = j - 1
ActiveSheet.Range("D" & TOTSTU + K & ":F" & TOTSTU + K).Merge
ActiveSheet.Range("D" & TOTSTU + K & ":F" & TOTSTU + K).Value = ActiveSheet.Range(Cells(i + 6, ((j - 1) * 3) + 6).Address)
ActiveSheet.Range("G" & TOTSTU + K & ":I" & TOTSTU + K).Merge
ActiveSheet.Range("G" & TOTSTU + K & ":I" & TOTSTU + K).Value = ActiveSheet.Range(Cells(i + 6, ((j - 1) * 3) + 7).Address)
ActiveSheet.Range("J" & TOTSTU + K & ":L" & TOTSTU + K).Merge
ActiveSheet.Range("J" & TOTSTU + K & ":L" & TOTSTU + K).Value = ActiveSheet.Range(Cells(i + 6, ((j - 1) * 3) + 8).Address)
ActiveSheet.Range("M" & TOTSTU + K & ":O" & TOTSTU + K).Merge
```

```
ActiveSheet.Range("M" & TOTSTU + K & ":O" & TOTSTU + K).Value =
ActiveSheet.Range(Cells(i + 6, ((j - 1) * 3) + 9).Address)
ActiveSheet.Range("D" & TOTSTU + K - 1 & ":O" & TOTSTU + K).Select
With Selection.Borders
.LineStyle = xlContinuous
.Weight = xlThin
End With
With Selection.Font
.Size = 11
End With
With Selection
.HorizontalAlignment = xlCenter
.VerticalAlignment = xlCenter
End With
K = K + 4
ActiveSheet.Range("B" & TOTSTU + K & ":E" & TOTSTU + K).Merge
ActiveSheet.Range("B" & TOTSTU + K & ":E" & TOTSTU + K).Value =
"PREPARED BY"
ActiveSheet.Range("F" & TOTSTU + K & ":I" & TOTSTU + K).Merge
ActiveSheet.Range("F" & TOTSTU + K & ":I" & TOTSTU + K).Value =
"CLASS TEACHER"
ActiveSheet.Range("J" & TOTSTU + K & ":M" & TOTSTU + K).Merge
ActiveSheet.Range("J" & TOTSTU + K & ":M" & TOTSTU + K).Value =
"CHAIRPERSON"
ActiveSheet.Range("N" & TOTSTU + K & ":Q" & TOTSTU + K).Merge
ActiveSheet.Range("N" & TOTSTU + K & ":Q" & TOTSTU + K).Value =
"PRINCIPAL"
ActiveSheet.Range("B" & TOTSTU + K & ":Q" & TOTSTU + K).Select
With Selection.Font
.Size = 12
End With
With Selection
.HorizontalAlignment = xlCenter
.VerticalAlignment = xlCenter
End With
s = s & "$B$" & Trim(Str(TOTSTU + M)) & ":$Q$" & Trim(Str(TOTSTU + K))
& ","
K = K + 4
```

```
Next
s = Left(s, Len(s) - 1)
ActiveSheet.PageSetup.PrintArea = s
End Sub
```

9

Print Invoice Format and Formulas

Sub Print_Invoice_Format_and_Formulas()

‘This Macro inserts a new Sheet and there it sets design, format and formulas for Ready-to-Print Invoice.

```
'SETTING COLUMNS WIDTH AND ROWS HEIGHT
Sheets.Add After:=Sheets(Sheets.COUNT)
Sheets(Sheets.COUNT).Activate
Range("A1").ColumnWidth = 0.58
Range("B1").ColumnWidth = 2.29
Range("C1").ColumnWidth = 14
Range("D1, S1").ColumnWidth = 5
Range("E1, F1").ColumnWidth = 4
Range("G1").ColumnWidth = 6.43
Range("H1").ColumnWidth = 4.14
Range("I1").ColumnWidth = 6.75
Range("J1").ColumnWidth = 8.43
Range("K1, M1, O1, Q1").ColumnWidth = 2.57
Range("L1, N1, P1, R1").ColumnWidth = 6
Range("T1").ColumnWidth = 8.86
Range("U1").ColumnWidth = 19.29
Range("V1").ColumnWidth = 19.29
Range("A1").RowHeight = 11.25
Range("A2, A17, A36, A41, A43:A47, A49:A50").RowHeight = 15
```

```
Range("A3").RowHeight = 22.25
Range("A4, A5, A16, A37:A40").RowHeight = 17.25
Range("A6:A7, A9, A11:A15, A18").RowHeight = 16.5
Range("A8").RowHeight = 23.5
Range("A10").RowHeight = 14.25
Range("A19:A22").RowHeight = 15
Range("A23").RowHeight = 40.5
Range("A24:A35").RowHeight = 30
Range("A42").RowHeight = 18.75
Range("A48").RowHeight = 7.5
Range("U4").VALUE = "Currency Name"
Range("U5").VALUE = "Currency Short Name"
Range("U6").VALUE = "Currency Symbol"
'SETTING PAGE SETUP
With ActiveSheet.PageSetup
.LeftMargin = Application.InchesToPoints(0.2)
.RightMargin = Application.InchesToPoints(0)
.TopMargin = Application.InchesToPoints(0.25)
.BottomMargin = Application.InchesToPoints(0)
.HeaderMargin = Application.InchesToPoints(0.3)
.FooterMargin = Application.InchesToPoints(0.3)
.PrintHeadings = False
.PrintGridlines = False
.PrintComments = xlPrintNoComments
.PrintQuality = 600
.CenterHorizontally = False
.CenterVertically = False
.Orientation = xlPortrait
.Draft = False
.PaperSize = xlPaperA4
.FirstPageNumber = xlAutomatic
.Order = xlDownThenOver
.BlackAndWhite = False
.Zoom = 85
.PrintErrors = xlPrintErrorsDisplayed
.ScaleWithDocHeaderFooter = True
.AlignMarginsHeaderFooter = True
End With
```

```
'DOING FORMATTING
Range("A1:T50").Select
With Selection
.HorizontalAlignment = xlCenter
.VerticalAlignment = xlCenter
.WrapText = False
End With
With Selection.Font
.Name = "Arial Unicode MS"
.Size = 12
.Strikethrough = False
.Superscript = False
.Subscript = False
.OutlineFont = False
.Shadow = False
.Underline = xlUnderlineStyleNone
.ThemeColor = xlThemeColorLight1
.TintAndShade = 0
.ThemeFont = xlThemeFontNone
End With
Range("B23:T23, C24:C35, F24:F35, D18:J19, N18:T19, B38:I39, L41:T42").Select
With Selection
.WrapText = True
End With
Range("B2:T2, B3:T3, B4:T4, B5:T5, B6:C6, D6:F6, G6:I6, J6:L6, M6:P6, Q6:T6, B7:C7, D7:F7, G7:I7, J7:L7, M7:P7, Q7:T7, B8:C8, D8:T8, B9:C9, D9:J9, K9:M9, N9:P9, B10:T10").Merge
Range("B11:T11, B12:C12, D12:G12, H12:I12, J12:M12, N12:Q12, R12:T12, B13:C13, D13:G13, H13:I13, J13:M13, N13:Q13, R13:T13, B14:C14, D14:G14, H14:I14, J14:M14, N14:Q14, R14:T14").Merge
Range("B15:C15, D15:G15, H15:I15, J15:M15, N15:Q15, R15:T15, B16:H16, J16:T16, B17:C17, D17:J17, K17:M17, N17:T17, B18:C18, D18:J19, K18:M18, N18:T19, B20:C20, D20:J20, K20:M20, N20:T20").Merge
Range("B21:C21, D21:J21, K21:M21, N21:T21, B22:C22, D22:G22, H22:I22, K22:M22, N22:Q22, R22:S22, K36:L36, M36:N36, O36:P36, Q36:R36").Merge
Range("B37:C37, J37:O37, P37:T37, B38:I39, J38:O38, P38:T38, J39:O39, P39:T39, B40:C40, D40:I40, J40:O40, P40:T40, L41:T42, B46:D46, L46:T46,
```

```
B47:E47, F47:I47, J47:O47, P47:T47, B49:T49").Merge
    Range("B2:T2, B6:T7, D18:J19, N18:T19, P37:P40, B46:T47").Select
    With Selection.Font
    .Size = 10
    End With
    Range("Q7:T7").Select
    With Selection.Font
    .Size = 8
    End With
    Range("B46, L46").Select
    With Selection
    .VerticalAlignment = xlTop
    End With
    Range("B2").VALUE = "Subject to XXX jurisdiction"
    Range("B16, J16, D17, N17, B23:T23, D36:T36, D40, P37:P40, B38, L41, B46,
L46, B49").Select
    Selection.Font.Bold = True
    Range("B3:T3").Select
    Selection.Font.Bold = True
    With Selection.Font
    .Size = 16
    End With
    Range("B3").VALUE = "Your Company Name"
    Range("B16:T16").Select
    With Selection.Font
    .Size = 13
    End With
    Range("B23:T23").Select
    With Selection.Font
    .Size = 7.5
    End With
    Range("B4:T4").Select
    Range("B4").VALUE = "Your Company Address Line 1"
    Range("B5:T5").Select
    Range("B5").VALUE = "Address Line 2"
    Range("B8:T15, B17:B22, D17, D20:D22, K17:K22, N17, N20:N22, B37:O40,
L41").Select
    With Selection.Font
```

```
.Size = 11
End With
Range("B24:T36").Select
With Selection.Font
.Size = 7
End With
Range("B6:T7").Select
With Selection
.VerticalAlignment = xlTop
End With
Range("B6").VALUE = "PHONE NO."
Range("D6").VALUE = "FSSAI NO."
Range("G6").VALUE = "PAN"
Range("J6").VALUE = "GSTIN"
Range("M6").VALUE = "TAN"
Range("Q6").VALUE = "EMAIL"
Range("B8:T9, B12:T15, B17:T22, C24:C35, B37, B40, J37:J40, B47:T47").Select
With Selection
.HorizontalAlignment = xlLeft
End With
Range("B8:T8").Select
With Selection
.VerticalAlignment = xlBottom
End With
Range("B8").VALUE = "IRN:"
Range("B9").VALUE = "ACK. NO."
Range("K9").VALUE = "ACK. DATE"
Range("B10").VALUE = "C R E D I T"
Range("B11").VALUE = "SAY BILL OF SUPPLY OR TAX INVOICE"
Range("B11:C11").Select
Selection.Font.Bold = True
Range("B12").VALUE = "Invoice No."
Range("H12").VALUE = "Veh No."
Range("N12").VALUE = "Owner’s PAN"
Range("B13").VALUE = "Invoice Date"
Range("H13").VALUE = "Owner"
Range("N13").VALUE = "Transporter"
Range("B14").VALUE = "State"
```

```
Range("H14").VALUE = "Driver"
Range("N14").VALUE = "Transporter GST"
Range("B15").VALUE = "State Code"
Range("H15").VALUE = "DL No."
Range("N15").VALUE = "Transporter PH"
Range("B16").VALUE = "BILL TO PARTY"
Range("J16").VALUE = "DELIVER TO PARTY"
Range("B17, K17").VALUE = "Name"
Range("B18, K18").VALUE = "Address"
Range("B20, K20").VALUE = "Place"
Range("B21, K21").VALUE = "GSTIN"
Range("B22, K22").VALUE = "State"
Range("H22, R22").VALUE = "St Code"
Range("B11:T49, B17:J22").Select
Selection.Borders(xlDiagonalDown).LineStyle = xlNone
Selection.Borders(xlDiagonalUp).LineStyle = xlNone
With Selection.Borders(xlEdgeLeft)
.LineStyle = xlContinuous
.ColorIndex = 0
.TintAndShade = 0
.Weight = xlThin
End With
With Selection.Borders(xlEdgeTop)
.LineStyle = xlContinuous
.ColorIndex = 0
.TintAndShade = 0
.Weight = xlThin
End With
With Selection.Borders(xlEdgeBottom)
.LineStyle = xlContinuous
.ColorIndex = 0
.TintAndShade = 0
.Weight = xlThin
End With
With Selection.Borders(xlEdgeRight)
.LineStyle = xlContinuous
.ColorIndex = 0
.TintAndShade = 0
```

```
.Weight = xlThin
End With
Selection.Borders(xlInsideVertical).LineStyle = xlNone
Selection.Borders(xlInsideHorizontal).LineStyle = xlNone
Range("B5:T5, B7:T7, B9:T9, B11:T11, B15:T15, B16:T16, B23:T23, B35:T35, B37:I37, R37:T37, R38:T38, R39:T39, B39:I39, B40:T40, B46:T46, B47:T47, B48:T48").Select
Selection.Borders(xlDiagonalDown).LineStyle = xlNone
Selection.Borders(xlDiagonalUp).LineStyle = xlNone
With Selection.Borders(xlEdgeBottom)
.LineStyle = xlContinuous
.ColorIndex = 0
.TintAndShade = 0
.Weight = xlThin
End With
Range("J37:O40, F47:I47, F47:I47, J47:O47").Select
Selection.Borders(xlDiagonalDown).LineStyle = xlNone
Selection.Borders(xlDiagonalUp).LineStyle = xlNone
With Selection.Borders(xlEdgeLeft)
.LineStyle = xlContinuous
.ColorIndex = 0
.TintAndShade = 0
.Weight = xlThin
End With
With Selection.Borders(xlEdgeRight)
.LineStyle = xlContinuous
.ColorIndex = 0
.TintAndShade = 0
.Weight = xlThin
End With
Range("B23:T36").Select
Selection.Borders(xlDiagonalDown).LineStyle = xlNone
Selection.Borders(xlDiagonalUp).LineStyle = xlNone
With Selection.Borders(xlEdgeLeft)
.LineStyle = xlContinuous
.ColorIndex = 0
.TintAndShade = 0
.Weight = xlThin
```

```
End With
With Selection.Borders(xlEdgeTop)
.LineStyle = xlContinuous
.ColorIndex = 0
.TintAndShade = 0
.Weight = xlThin
End With
With Selection.Borders(xlEdgeBottom)
.LineStyle = xlContinuous
.ColorIndex = 0
.TintAndShade = 0
.Weight = xlThin
End With
With Selection.Borders(xlEdgeRight)
.LineStyle = xlContinuous
.ColorIndex = 0
.TintAndShade = 0
.Weight = xlThin
End With
With Selection.Borders(xlInsideVertical)
.LineStyle = xlContinuous
.ColorIndex = 0
.TintAndShade = 0
.Weight = xlThin
End With
'SETTING FORMAT CELL
Range("B7:T7, D8, D9, R15, D24:D35").NumberFormat = "@"
Range("N9, D13").NumberFormat = "dd/mm/yyyy"
Range("G24:G36, I24:J36, L24:L35, K36, N24:N35, M36, P24:P35, O36, R24:R35, Q36, S24:S36, T24:T36, R37:R40, D40").Select
Selection.NumberFormat = "0.00"
Range("M24:M35, O24:O35, Q24:Q35").Select
Selection.NumberFormat = "0.0"
'SETTING ITEMS, RATE, TAX, AMOUNT DETAILS
Range("B23").VALUE = "Sl No"
Range("C23").VALUE = "Product Description"
Range("D23").VALUE = "HSN"
Range("E23").VALUE = "Qty."
```

```
Range("F23").VALUE = "Unit"
Range("G23").VALUE = "Unit Price"
Range("H23").VALUE = "Free Unit"
Range("I23").VALUE = "Disc. Amt."
Range("J23").VALUE = "Taxable Amt."
Range("K23").VALUE = "IGST%"
Range("L23").VALUE = "IGST Amt."
Range("M23").VALUE = "CGST%"
Range("N23").VALUE = "CGST Amt."
Range("O23").VALUE = "SGST%"
Range("P23").VALUE = "SGST Amt."
Range("Q23").VALUE = "GST%"
Range("R23").VALUE = "GST Amt."
Range("S23").VALUE = "Oth. Chrgs."
Range("T23").VALUE = "TOTAL Amt."
'SETTING FORMULA TO CELLS
Cells(24, 9).Formula = "=G24*H24"
Cells(24, 10).Formula = "=E24*G24-I24"
Cells(24, 12).Formula = "=J24*K24%"
Cells(24, 14).Formula = "=J24*M24%"
Cells(24, 16).Formula = "=J24*O24%"
Cells(24, 17).Formula = "=O24+M24+K24"
Cells(24, 18).Formula = "=L24+N24+P24"
Cells(24, 20).Formula = "=J24+R24+S24"
Dim I As Integer
I = 0
For I = 73 To 84
If I <> 75 And I <> 77 And I <> 79 And I <> 83 Then
Range(Chr(I) & 24).Select
Selection.AutoFill Destination:=Range(Chr(I) & 24 & ":" & Chr(I) & 35),
Type:=xlFillDefault
End If
Next
Range("D36").VALUE = "TOTAL"
Range("E36").Formula = "=ROUND(SUM(E24:E35),2)"
Range("H36").Formula = "=ROUND(SUM(H24:H35),2)"
Range("I36").Formula = "=ROUND(SUM(I24:I35),2)"
Range("J36").Formula = "=ROUND(SUM(J24:J35),2)"
```

```
Range("K36").Formula = "=ROUND(SUM(L24:L35),2)"
Range("M36").Formula = "=ROUND(SUM(N24:N35),2)"
Range("O36").Formula = "=ROUND(SUM(P24:P35),2)"
Range("Q36").Formula = "=ROUND(K36,2) + ROUND(M36,2) + ROUND(O36,2)"
Range("S36").Formula = "=ROUND(SUM(S24:S35),2)"
Range("T36").Formula = "=ROUND(J36,2) + ROUND(K36,2) + ROUND(M36,2) + ROUND(O36,2) + ROUND(S36,2)"
Range("B37").VALUE = "Amount in Words"
Range("J37").VALUE = "Taxable Amt --||-- GST Amt"
Range("P37").Formula = "=ROUND(J36, 2) & "" --||-- "" & ROUND(Q36, 2)"
Range("J38").VALUE = "Other Charges"
Range("P38").Formula = "=S36"
Range("J39").VALUE = "TCS Amount @ 0.1%"
Range("P39").Formula = "=T36*0.1%"
Range("J40").VALUE = "Rounding Off"
Range("P40").Formula = "=((T36+P39)-ROUND(T36+P39,0))*-1"
If Range("U4").VALUE = "" Then Range("U4").VALUE = "Currency Name"
If Range("U5").VALUE = "" Then Range("U5").VALUE = "Currency Short Name"
If Range("U6").VALUE = "" Then Range("U6").VALUE = "Currency Symbol"
If Range("V4").VALUE = "" Then Range("V4").VALUE = "US Dollar"
If Range("V5").VALUE = "" Then Range("V5").VALUE = "USD"
If Range("V6").VALUE = "" Then Range("V6").VALUE = "$"
Range("B40").VALUE = "Invoice Total"
Range("D40").Formula = "=V5 & "" "" & V6 & "" "" & IF(P40=0.50, ROUNDUP(T36+P39,0), ROUND(T36+P39,0))"
ActiveSheet.Range("U65").VALUE = "For"
For I = 1 To Len(ActiveSheet.Range("B3").VALUE)
ActiveSheet.Range("U65").VALUE = ActiveSheet.Range("U65").VALUE & "_"
Next
Range("L41").Formula = "=U65 & CHAR(10) & "" "" & B3"
Range("B46").VALUE = "Party's Signature"
Range("L46").VALUE = "Authorised Signatory"
Range("B47").VALUE = "Bank:"
Range("F47").VALUE = "IFSC:"
Range("J47").VALUE = "A/C:"
Range("P47").VALUE = "Branch:"
```

```
Range("B49").VALUE = "Original Copy For Recipient"
'SETTING NUMBER OF ITEMS
While (I < 1 Or I > 12)
s = InputBox("Enter Total number of Items in the Invoice.")
If IsNumeric(s) = True Then I = Int(s)
Wend
For J = 1 To I
Range("B" & 23 + J).VALUE = J
Next
If I < 12 Then
Range("C" & 24 + I & ":C35").Select
Selection.EntireRow.Delete
Range("B" & 24 + I & ":T" & 24 + I).Select
Selection.Borders(xlDiagonalDown).LineStyle = xlNone
Selection.Borders(xlDiagonalUp).LineStyle = xlNone
With Selection.Borders(xlEdgeTop)
.LineStyle = xlContinuous
.ColorIndex = 0
.TintAndShade = 0
.Weight = xlThin
End With
For J = 1 To (12 - I) * 2 - 1
Range("C" & 24 + I + 5).Select
Selection.EntireRow.Insert
Next
Range("C" & 24 + I + 5 & ":C" & 24 + I + 5 + (12 - I) * 2 - 1).RowHeight = 15
Range("C" & 24 + I + 10 + (12 - I) * 2 - 1).RowHeight = 30
ActiveSheet.PageSetup.PrintArea = "$A$1:$T$" & 24 + I + 14 + (12 - I) * 2 - 1
Else
Range("B36:T36").Select
Selection.Borders(xlDiagonalDown).LineStyle = xlNone
Selection.Borders(xlDiagonalUp).LineStyle = xlNone
With Selection.Borders(xlEdgeTop)
.LineStyle = xlContinuous
.ColorIndex = 0
.TintAndShade = 0
.Weight = xlThin
End With
```

```
ActiveSheet.PageSetup.PrintArea = "$A$1:$T$50"
End If
MsgBox ("After you have entered Invoice details etc, please Run the Macro named ""Amount_in_Words"" to get the Amount in Words.")
Range("B2").Select
End Sub
```

10

Amount in Words

Sub Amount_in_Words()

'This Macro is written for Macro "Ready_to_Print_Invoice... for getting the amount in words. But it works independently too."

```
    On Error GoTo ERR
    Dim S1(30), s(11), RS, rs1, SS, RUPEE, inputrow, outputrow As String
    RUPEE = ""
    RS = ""
    S1(0) = "One "
    S1(1) = "Two "
    S1(2) = "Three "
    S1(3) = "Four "
    S1(4) = "Five "
    S1(5) = "Six "
    S1(6) = "Seven "
    S1(7) = "Eight "
    S1(8) = "Nine "
    S1(9) = "Ten "
    S1(10) = "Eleven "
    S1(11) = "Twelve "
    S1(12) = "Thirteen "
    S1(13) = "Fourteen "
    S1(14) = "Fifteen "
    S1(15) = "Sixteen "
    S1(16) = "Seventeen "
```

```
S1(17) = "Eighteen "
S1(18) = "Nineteen "
S1(19) = "Twenty "
S1(20) = "Thirty "
S1(21) = "Forty "
S1(22) = "Fifty "
S1(23) = "Sixty "
S1(24) = "Seventy "
S1(25) = "Eighty "
S1(26) = "Ninety "
S1(27) = "Hundred "
S1(28) = "Thousand "
S1(29) = "Lacs "
For I = 24 To 40
If ActiveSheet.Range("B" & I).VALUE = "Invoice Total" Then
If ActiveSheet.Range("B2").Formula = "=LEFT(U2,11) & V2 & RIGHT(U2,13)" And (ActiveSheet.Range("D" & I).Formula = "=V63 & "" "" & V64 & "" "" & IF(P" & Trim(Str(I)) & "=0.5, ROUNDUP(T" & Trim(Str(I - 4)) & "+P" & Trim(Str(I - 1)) & ",0), ROUND(T" & Trim(Str(I - 4)) & "+P" & Trim(Str(I - 1)) & ",0))" Or ActiveSheet.Range("D" & I).Formula = "=V63&"" ""&V64&"" ""&IF(P" & Trim(Str(I)) & "=0.5, ROUNDUP(T" & Trim(Str(I - 4)) & "+P" & Trim(Str(I - 1)) & ",0), ROUND(T" & Trim(Str(I - 4)) & "+P" & Trim(Str(I - 1)) & ",0))") Then
SS = Right(ActiveSheet.Range("D" & I).VALUE, Len(ActiveSheet.Range("D" & I).VALUE) - (Len(ActiveSheet.Range("V63").VALUE) + Len(ActiveSheet.Range("V64").VALUE) + 2))
ElseIf ActiveSheet.Range("I24").Formula = "=G24*H24" And ActiveSheet.Range("J24").Formula = "=E24*G24-I24" And ActiveSheet.Range("L24").Formula = "=J24*K24%" And ActiveSheet.Range("N24").Formula = "=J24*M24%" And ActiveSheet.Range("B10").VALUE = "C R E D I T" And (ActiveSheet.Range("D" & I).Formula = "=V5&"" ""&V6&"" ""&IF(P" & Trim(Str(I)) & "=0.5, ROUNDUP(T" & Trim(Str(I - 4)) & "+P" & Trim(Str(I - 1)) & ",0), ROUND(T" & Trim(Str(I - 4)) & "+P" & Trim(Str(I - 1)) & ",0))" Or ActiveSheet.Range("D" & I).Formula = "=V5 & "" "" & V6 & "" "" & IF(P" & Trim(Str(I)) & "=0.5, ROUNDUP(T" & Trim(Str(I - 4)) & "+P" & Trim(Str(I - 1)) & ",0), ROUND(T" & Trim(Str(I - 4)) & "+P" & Trim(Str(I - 1)) & ",0))") Then
SS = Right(ActiveSheet.Range("D" & I).VALUE, Len(ActiveSheet.Range("D" & I).VALUE) - (Len(ActiveSheet.Range("V5").VALUE) +
```

```
Len(ActiveSheet.Range("V6").VALUE) + 2))
    Else
    SS = ActiveSheet.Range("D" & I).VALUE
    End If
    outputrow = "B" & I - 2
    outputrow = Trim(outputrow)
    Exit For
    End If
    Next
    If IsNumeric(SS) = False Then SS = ""
    If SS = "" Then
    inputrow = InputBox("Enter Input Cell Address of Amount in digits.")
    SS = ActiveSheet.Range(inputrow).VALUE
    outputrow = InputBox("Enter Output Cell Address for Amount in words.")
    End If
    SS = Trim(SS)
    RUPEE = ""
    RS = Int(SS)
    If Len(RS) > 7 Then
    rs1 = Left(RS, Len(RS) - 7)
    RS = Right(RS, 7)
    End If
    If Len(rs1) > 7 Then rs1 = Right(rs1, 7)
    PART2:
    If Len(RS) = 7 Then
    If Int(Left(RS, 1)) = 1 Then
    s(0) = S1(Int(Mid(RS, 2, 1)) + 9)
    ElseIf Int(Left(RS, 1)) > 1 Then
    s(0) = S1(Int(Left(RS, 1)) + 17)
    If Int(Mid(RS, 2, 1)) <> 0 Then s(1) = S1(Int(Mid(RS, 2, 1)) - 1)
    Else
    If Int(Mid(RS, 2, 1)) <> 0 Then s(1) = S1(Int(Mid(RS, 2, 1)) - 1)
    End If
    If s(0) <> "" Or s(1) <> "" Then s(2) = S1(29)
    End If
    If Len(RS) = 6 Then
    If Int(Left(RS, 1)) > 0 Then
    s(0) = S1(Int(Left(RS, 1)) - 1)
```

```
s(1) = S1(29)
End If
End If
If Len(RS) > 4 Then
If Int(Left(Right(RS, 5), 1)) = 1 Then
s(3) = S1(Int(Left(Right(RS, 4), 1)) + 9)
ElseIf Int(Left(Right(RS, 5), 1)) > 1 Then
s(3) = S1(Left(Right(RS, 5), 1) + 17)
If Int(Left(Right(RS, 4), 1)) <> 0 Then s(4) = S1(Int(Left(Right(RS, 4), 1)) - 1)
Else
If Int(Left(Right(RS, 4), 1)) <> 0 Then s(4) = S1(Int(Left(Right(RS, 4), 1)) - 1)
End If
If s(3) <> "" Or s(4) <> "" Then s(5) = S1(28)
End If
If Len(RS) = 4 Then
If Int(Left(RS, 1)) > 0 Then
s(0) = S1(Int(Left(RS, 1)) - 1)
s(1) = S1(28)
End If
End If
If Len(RS) > 2 Then
If Int(Left(Right(RS, 3), 1)) <> 0 Then
s(6) = S1(Int(Left(Right(RS, 3), 1)) - 1)
s(7) = S1(27)
End If
End If
If Len(RS) > 1 Then
If Int(Left(Right(RS, 2), 1)) = 1 Then
s(8) = S1(Int(Left(Right(RS, 1), 1)) + 9)
ElseIf Int(Left(Right(RS, 2), 1)) > 1 Then
s(8) = S1(Left(Right(RS, 2), 1) + 17)
If Int(Left(Right(RS, 1), 1)) <> 0 Then s(9) = S1(Int(Left(Right(RS, 1), 1)) - 1)
Else
If Int(Left(Right(RS, 1), 1)) <> 0 Then s(9) = S1(Int(Left(Right(RS, 1), 1)) - 1)
End If
End If
If Len(RS) = 1 Then
If Int(Left(RS, 1)) > 0 Then s(0) = S1(Int(Left(RS, 1)) - 1)
```

```
End If
RS = ""
RS = s(0) & s(1) & s(2) & s(3) & s(4) & s(5) & s(6) & s(7) & s(8) & s(9)
If RUPEE = "" Then
RUPEE = RS
Else
RUPEE = RS & "Crore " & RUPEE
End If
RUPEE = Trim(RUPEE)
If ActiveSheet.Range("B2").Formula = "=LEFT(U2,11) & V2 & RIGHT(U2,13)" And (ActiveSheet.Range("D" & I).Formula = "=V63 & "" "" & V64 & "" "" & IF(P" & Trim(Str(I)) & "=0.5, ROUNDUP(T" & Trim(Str(I - 4)) & "+P" & Trim(Str(I - 1)) & ",0), ROUND(T" & Trim(Str(I - 4)) & "+P" & Trim(Str(I - 1)) & ",0))" Or ActiveSheet.Range("D" & I).Formula = "=V63&"" ""&V64&"" ""&IF(P" & Trim(Str(I)) & "=0.5, ROUNDUP(T" & Trim(Str(I - 4)) & "+P" & Trim(Str(I - 1)) & ",0), ROUND(T" & Trim(Str(I - 4)) & "+P" & Trim(Str(I - 1)) & ",0))") Then
If RUPEE <> "" Then ActiveSheet.Range(outputrow).VALUE = ActiveSheet.Range("V62").VALUE & " " & RUPEE & " Only."
ElseIf ActiveSheet.Range("I24").Formula = "=G24*H24" And ActiveSheet.Range("J24").Formula = "=E24*G24-I24" And ActiveSheet.Range("L24").Formula = "=J24*K24%" And ActiveSheet.Range("N24").Formula = "=J24*M24%" And ActiveSheet.Range("B10").VALUE = "C R E D I T" And (ActiveSheet.Range("D" & I).Formula = "=V5&"" ""&V6&"" ""&IF(P" & Trim(Str(I)) & "=0.5, ROUNDUP(T" & Trim(Str(I - 4)) & "+P" & Trim(Str(I - 1)) & ",0), ROUND(T" & Trim(Str(I - 4)) & "+P" & Trim(Str(I - 1)) & ",0))" Or ActiveSheet.Range("D" & I).Formula = "=V5 & "" "" & V6 & "" "" & IF(P" & Trim(Str(I)) & "=0.5, ROUNDUP(T" & Trim(Str(I - 4)) & "+P" & Trim(Str(I - 1)) & ",0), ROUND(T" & Trim(Str(I - 4)) & "+P" & Trim(Str(I - 1)) & ",0))") Then
If RUPEE <> "" Then ActiveSheet.Range(outputrow).VALUE = ActiveSheet.Range("V4").VALUE & " " & RUPEE & " Only."
Else
If RUPEE <> "" Then ActiveSheet.Range(outputrow).VALUE = RUPEE & " Only."
End If
For I = 0 To 9
s(I) = ""
Next I
```

```
RS = rs1
rs1 = ""
If Len(RS) > 0 Then GoTo PART2
Exit Sub
ERR:
MsgBox ERR.Number & " " & ERR.Description
End Sub
```

11

Encode the Sheet 100 Cols 100 Rows

Sub Encode_the_Sheet_100_Cols_100_Rows()

```
On Error GoTo ERR
    Dim S1, S2 As Variant
    Dim change(20), CHANGE2(20), l, M As Integer
    Dim J, k As Long
    Workbooks("PLAY WITH EXCEL.xlsm").Worksheets("Sheet1").Activate
    Workbooks("PLAY WITH EXCEL.xlsm").Worksheets("Sheet1").Range("A1").Select
    For I = 1 To 20
    If I < 11 Then
    change(I - 1) = I * I
    CHANGE2(I - 1) = I * 4
    Else
    change(I - 1) = I * 3
    CHANGE2(I - 1) = I * 2
    End If
    Next
    M = 0
    For J = 1 To 100
    For k = 1 To 100
    S1 = ""
    S1 = """" & Sheets("Sheet1").Cells(J, k).NumberFormat & """"
```

```
S1 = S1 & Sheets("Sheet1").Cells(J, k).VALUE
Sheets("Sheet1").Cells(J, k).NumberFormat = "General"
S2 = """"
l = 0
For I = 1 To Len(S1)
S2 = S2 & Chr(Asc(Mid(S1, I, 1)) + change(l) + CHANGE2(M))
l = l + 1
If l > 19 Then l = 0
Next
M = M + 1
If M > 19 Then M = 0
Sheets("Sheet1").Cells(J, k).VALUE = S2
Next
Next
Exit Sub
ERR:
MsgBox ERR.Number & " " & ERR.Description
End Sub
```

12

Decode the Sheet 100 Cols 100 Rows

Sub Decode_the_Sheet_100_Cols_100_Rows()

```
On Error GoTo ERR
    Dim S1, S2, s3 As Variant
    Dim change(20), CHANGE2(20), l, M As Integer
    Dim J, k As Long
    Workbooks("PLAY WITH EXCEL.xlsm").Worksheets("Sheet1").Activate
    Workbooks("PLAY WITH EXCEL.xlsm").Worksheets("Sheet1").Range("A1").Select
    For I = 1 To 20
    If I < 11 Then
    change(I - 1) = I * I
    CHANGE2(I - 1) = I * 4
    Else
    change(I - 1) = I * 3
    CHANGE2(I - 1) = I * 2
    End If
    Next
    M = 0
    For J = 1 To 100
    For k = 1 To 100
    S1 = ""
    S1 = Sheets("Sheet1").Cells(J, k).VALUE
```

```
S2 = ""
l = 0
For I = 2 To Len(S1)
S2 = S2 & Chr(Asc(Mid(S1, I, 1)) - (change(l) + CHANGE2(M)))
l = l + 1
If l > 19 Then l = 0
Next
'If Left(S2, 1) <> """" Then
'MsgBox "Data of " & Cells(J, k).Address & " is either not Encoded or it is corrupted."
'End If
For I = 2 To Len(S2)
If Mid(S2, I, 1) = """" Then
s3 = Mid(S2, 2, I - 2)
S1 = Right(S2, Len(S2) - I)
Exit For
End If
Next
'If I > Len(S2) Then
'MsgBox "Data of " & Cells(J, k).Address & " is either not Encoded or it is corrupted."
'End If
M = M + 1
If M > 19 Then M = 0
If Left(S2, 1) = """" And I <= Len(S2) Then
Sheets("Sheet1").Cells(J, k).VALUE = S1
Sheets("Sheet1").Cells(J, k).Select
Selection.NumberFormat = s3
End If
Next
Next
Exit Sub
ERR:
MsgBox ERR.Number & " " & ERR.Description
End Sub
```

13

Square Roots Up To 15 Decimal Places

Sub Square_Roots_Up_To_15Decimal_Places()

```
'This Macro finds Square Roots (up to 15 Decimal Places) of Numbers present in Cells B2 to B20 and gives result in Cells C2 to C20.
'So you just need to enter numbers in Cells B2 to B20 for which you want Square Roots. For blank cells it will give zero as result.
Dim n, n1, dec As Double
ActiveSheet.Range("B1").Value = "VALUES"
ActiveSheet.Range("C1").Value = "SQUARE ROOT"
For j = 2 To 20
i = 0
If IsNumeric(ActiveSheet.Range("B" & j).Value) Then
n = ActiveSheet.Range("B" & j).Value
Else
n = 0
End If
n1 = n
While (i = 0)
n1 = Int(n1 / 2)
If (n1 * n1) <= Val(n) Then
ln = n1
hn = n1 * 2
i = 1
```

```
End If
Wend
For i = 2 To 10000
If ((hn - Int(hn / i)) * (hn - Int(hn / i))) > Val(n) Then hn = hn - Int(hn / i)
If hn - ln < 10 Then Exit For
Next
For i = 2 To 10000
If ((ln + Int(ln / i)) * (ln + Int(ln / i))) < Val(n) Then ln = ln + Int(ln / i)
If hn - ln < 10 Then Exit For
Next
i = 1
If (n - (ln * ln)) >= ((hn * hn) - n) Then
While (i = 1)
If (hn * hn) <= Val(n) Then
i = 0
n1 = hn
End If
hn = hn - 1
Wend
Else
While (i = 1)
If (ln * ln) > Val(n) Then
i = 0
n1 = ln - 1
End If
ln = ln + 1
Wend
End If
dec = 0
ten = 10
REP:
If (n1 + dec) * (n1 + dec) = Val(n) Then GoTo REP1
If (n1 + dec) * (n1 + dec) > Val(n) Then
dec = dec - 1 / ten
ten = ten * 10
End If
dec = dec + 1 / ten
If (ten < 1E+16) Then GoTo REP
```

```
REP1:
ActiveSheet.Range("C" & j).Value = n1 + dec
Next
End Sub
```

14

Copy Records of Selected ID to Sheet2

Sub Copy_Records_of_Selected_ID_to_Sheet2()

‘If you have a Data Sheet in Sheet1 which have many records and you want all records of particular IDs or Names or anything to be copied in Sheet2.

'You need to select those IDs or Names or Anything [in First Column] - If an ID has multiple rows, you need to select just one place

‘Suppose your Datasheet Range in Sheet1 is A1:Z1000

'One ID ‘Apple’ has 25 entries in Row 15 and 24 other rows

‘Another ID 'Orange‘ has 17 entries in Rows 23 and 16 other rows

'You need to select Orange and Apple in any rows - Ex. A15 AND A17

'Then run this Macro. It will copy 25 records of Apple and then 17 records of Orange in Sheet2

```
Dim i As Long
Dim rec, K As Integer
Dim s, s2, id As String
id = ""
rec = 0
K = 1
i = 1
Worksheets("Sheet1").Activate
For Each cell In Selection
s = s & cell & ","
Next
```

```
s2 = ""
For j = 1 To Len(s)
If Mid(s, j, 1) = "," Then
id = Mid(s, K, j - K)
i = 0
While (Worksheets("Sheet1").Range("A" & i).Value <> "")
Worksheets("Sheet1").Activate
If Worksheets("Sheet1").Range("A" & i).Value = id Then
rec = rec + 1
s2 = Trim(Str(i)) & ":" & Trim(Str(i))
ROWS(s2).Select
Selection.Copy
Worksheets("Sheet2").Activate
Worksheets("Sheet2").Range("A" & rec).Select
ActiveCell.PasteSpecial
End If
i = i + 1
Wend
K = j + 1
End If
Next j
Application.CutCopyMode = False
End Sub
```

15

Code for Manipulating Data

Sub Code_for_Manipulating_Data()

```
'Suppose you have Data in Range A2:f1000
'Data has multiple records of some Uniqu IDs
'This Macro will copy 4-4 random records of each Ids and will paste in same Sheet in Columns I to N
'To check you simply type ab and cd in cells from A2 to A10 and any numbers or strings in cells from B2 to B10 and run this Macro.
Dim FR, LR As Long
Dim id(100), TROWS(100) As String
Dim RROW(4), KKK As Integer
KKK = 2
FR = 2
LR = 1000
For i = FR To LR
If ActiveSheet.Range("A" & i).Value = "" Then Exit For
For j = 0 To 99
If id(j) = "" Then
id(j) = ActiveSheet.Range("A" & i).Value
TROWS(j) = Trim(Str(i)) & ","
Exit For
ElseIf id(j) = ActiveSheet.Range("A" & i).Value Then
TROWS(j) = TROWS(j) & Trim(Str(i)) & ","
Exit For
End If
```

```
Next
Next
Dim K As Integer
For i = 0 To 99
K = 0
If id(i) = "" Then Exit For
For j = 1 To Len(TROWS(i))
If Mid(TROWS(i), j, 1) = "," Then K = K + 1
Next
For L = 0 To 3
Dim counter(4) As Integer
counter(0) = 0
counter(1) = 0
counter(2) = 0
counter(3) = 0
DOAGAIN:
RROW(L) = Int(1 + Rnd * (K - 1 + 1))
For M = 0 To L - 1
counter(L) = counter(L) + 1
If RROW(L) = RROW(M) And counter(L) < 10 Then GoTo DOAGAIN
Next
KK = 0
For n = 1 To Len(TROWS(i))
If Mid(TROWS(i), n, 1) = "," Then KK = KK + 1
If KK = RROW(L) And counter(L) < 10 Then
For II = n - 1 To 1 Step -1
If Mid(TROWS(i), II, 1) = "," Then
SS = Mid(TROWS(i), II + 1, n - (II + 1))
ActiveSheet.Range("I" & KKK & ":N" & KKK).Value = ActiveSheet.Range("A" & Int(SS) & ":F" & Int(SS)).Value
KKK = KKK + 1
Exit For
End If
If II = 1 Then
SS = Mid(TROWS(i), 1, n - (II))
ActiveSheet.Range("I" & KKK & ":N" & KKK).Value = ActiveSheet.Range("A" & Int(SS) & ":F" & Int(SS)).Value
KKK = KKK + 1
```

```
End If
Next
Exit For
End If
Next
Next
Next
End Sub
```

16

Find Palindromes in A Range

```
Sub Find_Palindromes_in_A_Range()

Dim n1, n2, i As Long
    Dim p As Long
    Dim s As String
    p = 3
    n1 = InputBox("Enter the Range Start.")
    n2 = InputBox("Enter the Range End.")
    ActiveSheet.Range("C1").Value = "List of Palindromes"
    ActiveSheet.Range("C2").Value = "Between " & n1 & " & " & n2
    For i = n1 To n2
    s = Trim(StrReverse(i))
    If s = Trim(Str(i)) Then
    ActiveSheet.Range("C" & p).Value = i
    p = p + 1
    End If
    Next
    ActiveSheet.Range("C" & p).Value = "Total " & p - 3 & " Palindromes are there between the Range " & n1 & " & " & n2
    End Sub
```

17

Find Palindrome of Whole or Decimal

Sub Find_Palindrome_ of_Whole_or_Decimal()

```
Dim n1 As Variant
    Dim s1 As String
    n1 = InputBox("Enter the Number.")
    If n1 = StrReverse(n1) Then
    MsgBox ("Yes! " & n1 & " is a Palindrome Number.")
    Else
    MsgBox ("No! " & n1 & " is not a Palindrome Number.")
    End If
    End Sub
```

18

Records having Common Filter Word

Sub Records_having_Common_Filter_Word()

```
'Suppose your Data Range is A1 to T20
'And it has a word 'Love' entered in more than one columns in more than one places
'Now if you want to see those data rows, which has the word 'Love' present in any Column
'You just need to run this Macro
i = MsgBox("Need to delete Data of Cells U1 to U20. Click on Yes if agree or else click on No", vbYesNo)
If i = 7 Then Exit Sub
ActiveSheet.Range("U1:U20").Value = ""
For i = 1 To 20
For j = 1 To 20
If UCase(Cells(j, i).Value) = "LOVE" Then
Cells(j, 21).Value = "LOVE"
End If
Next
Next
Range("A1:U20").Select
Selection.AutoFilter
ActiveSheet.Range("$A$1:$U$20").AutoFilter FIELD:=21, Criteria1:="LOVE"
End Sub
```

19

Create Inv Data for Json E Invoice

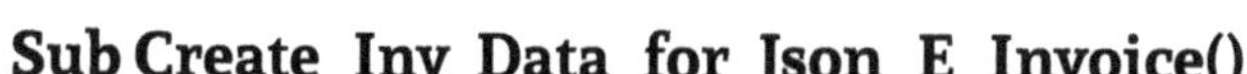

Sub Create_Inv_Data_for_Json_E_Invoice()

```
On Error GoTo ERR
    Dim s(11) As Variant
    Workbooks("PLAY WITH EXCEL.xlsm").Worksheets("Sheet1").Activate
    Workbooks("PLAY WITH EXCEL.xlsm").Worksheets("Sheet1").Range("A1").Select
    Workbooks("PLAY WITH EXCEL.xlsm").Worksheets("Sheet1").Range("A1:AZ50000").VALUE = ""
    s(0) = "INV NO+INV DATE+SELLER GSTIN+LEGAL NAME+ADDRESS1+ADDRESS2+LOCATION+PINCODE+STATE CODE+BUYER GSTIN+LEGAL NAME+PLACE OF SUPPLY+ADDRESS1+ADDRESS2+LOCATION+PINCODE+STATE CODE+SHIP-TO-GSTIN+LEGAL NAME+ADDRESS1+ADDRESS2+LOCATION+PINCODE+STATE CODE+HSN+PROD DES.+QTY+FREE QTY+UNIT+UNIT PRICE+DISCOUNT+TOT AMT+IGST AMT+CGST AMT+SGST AMT+TotItemVal+OTHER CHARGE+ROUND OFF+Transport ID+TransName+TransMode+Distance+TransDocNo+Trans DocDt+VehNo+VehType+Ship Dtls? Y/N+EwbDtls? Y/N+"
    s(1) = "T/T/R/101/20-21+24/1/2021+21XXXXXXXXXXXXX+XYZ1+ABC, DEF+GHI, JKL+MNO+100000+21+21YYYYYYYYYYYYY+XYZ2+21+PQR, STY+ZAB, CDE+DDD+200000+21+21YYYYYYYYYYYYY+XYZ2+FGI,
```

```
JKL+MNO, PQR+EEE+300000+21+1101+XXX ATTA 30
KG+150+15+BAG+900+13500+121500+0+2.5%+2.5%+127575+308.31+
    -0.31+21AAAAA1234A1A1+ABCD
TRANSPORT+1+30+++AB01CD1234+R+Y+Y+"
    'Please note s(1) upto abobe is single string, no line break.
    s(2) = "++++++++++++++++++++++++1101+XXX MAIDA 50
KG+200+0+BAG+1300+0+260000+0+2.5%+2.5%+273000+0+0++++++++++"
    s(3) = "++++++++++++++++++++++++6305+OLD GUNNY
BAGS+1000+0+PCS+10+0+10000+0+2.5%+2.5%+10500+0+0++++++++++"
    s(4) = "+++++++++++++++++++++++++++++++++++++++++++++++"
    s(5) = "T/T/R/075/20-21+20/1/2021+21XXXXXXXXXXXXX+XYZ1+ABC,
DEF+GHI, JKL+MNO+100000+21+37YYYYYYYYYYYYY+XYZ3+37+PQR,
STY2+ZAB, CDE2+DDD2+400000+37+37YYYYYYYYYYYYY+XYZ3+PQR,
STY2+ZAB, CDE2+DDD2+500000+37+1101+YYY SUJI 25
KG+50+0+BAG+800+0+40000+5%+0+0+42000+0+0+21BBBBB1234A1A1+EFGH
TRANSPORT+1+60+++CD01EF1234+R+N+Y+"
    s(6) = "+++++++++++++++++++++++++++++++++++++++++++++++"
    s(7) = "T/T/R/055/20-21+18/01/2021+21XXXXXXXXXXXXX+XYZ1+ABC,
DEF+GHI, JKL+MNO+100000+21+37YYYYYYYYYYYYY+XYZ3+37+PQR,
STY2+ZAB, CDE2+DDD2+400000+37+37YYYYYYYYYYYYY+XYZ3+PQR,
STY2+ZAB, CDE2+DDD2+500000+37+1101+ATTA 5
KG+3000+0+BAG+160+0+480000+
    18%+0+0+566400+0+0+21CCCCC1234A1A1+IJKL TRANSPORT+
    1+90+++GH01IJ1234+R+Y+N+"
    'Please note s(7) upto abobe is single string, no line break.
    s(8) = "+++++++++++++++++++++++++++++++++++++++++++++++"
    s(9) = "T/T/R/111/20-21+25/1/2021+21XXXXXXXXXXXXX+XYZ1+ABC,
DEF+GHI, JKL+MNO+100000+21+21YYYYYYYYYY11+XYZ3+21+PQR,
STY3+ZAB, CDE3+DDD3+600000+21+21YYYYYYYYYY11+XYZ23+FGI,
JKL3+MNO, PQR3+EEE3+600000+21+6305+OLD GUNNY
BAGS+5000+0+PCS+10+0+50000+0+6%+6%+56000+273.87+0.13+
    21DDDDD1234A1A1+MNOP TRANSPORT+1+100+++IJ01KL1234+R+N++"
    s(10) = "++++++++++++++++++++++++1101+XXX MAIDA 50
KG+200+0+BAG+1310+0+262000+0+9%+9%+309160+0+0++++++++++"
    'Please note s(9) upto abobe is single string, no line break.
    Dim I, J, k, l, N As Integer
    Dim S1(48) As Variant
    J = 0
```

```
k = 0
N = 0
l = 1
For I = 1 To 11
For J = 1 To Len(s(I - 1))
If Mid(s(I - 1), J, 1) = "+" Then
S1(N) = Mid(s(I - 1), l, k)
l = J + 1
k = 0
N = N + 1
Else
k = k + 1
End If
Next J
For J = 65 To 112
If J > 90 Then
Workbooks("PLAY WITH EXCEL.xlsm").Worksheets("Sheet1").Range("A" & Chr(J - 26) & I).VALUE = S1(J - 65)
Else
Workbooks("PLAY WITH EXCEL.xlsm").Worksheets("Sheet1").Range(Chr(J) & I).VALUE = S1(J - 65)
End If
Next J
k = 0
N = 0
l = 1
Next I
Workbooks("PLAY WITH EXCEL.xlsm").Worksheets("Sheet1").Range("A" & I).VALUE = "Above is Sample Data for creating Json file. You have to enter Invoice/s details in this format only. Remember to leave one blank row between each Invoice. When you are ready, please Run the Macro - CREATE_JSON_FILE_FOR_EINVOICE"
Workbooks("PLAY WITH EXCEL.xlsm").Worksheets("Sheet1").Range("AG2:AI11").Select
Selection.NumberFormat = "0.00%"
Workbooks("PLAY WITH EXCEL.xlsm").Worksheets("Sheet1").Range("A2").Select
Exit Sub
```

```
ERR:
MsgBox ERR.Number & " " & ERR.Description
End Sub
```

20

Create Json File for E Invoice

Sub Create_Json_File_for_E_Invoice()

```
On Error GoTo ERR
    Dim I, J, k, SL, COUNT As Integer
    Dim II As Long
    Dim D, M, Y As String
    Dim ASSVAL, IGST, CGST, SGST As Double
    I = 1
    Workbooks("PLAY WITH EXCEL.xlsm").Worksheets("Sheet1").Activate
    Workbooks("PLAY WITH EXCEL.xlsm").Worksheets("Sheet1").Range("A1").Select
    If Workbooks("PLAY WITH EXCEL.xlsm").Worksheets("Sheet1").Range("A1").VALUE <> "INV NO" Or Workbooks("PLAY WITH EXCEL.xlsm").Worksheets("Sheet1").Range("B1").VALUE <> "INV DATE" Or Workbooks("PLAY WITH EXCEL.xlsm").Worksheets("Sheet1").Range("C1").VALUE <> "SELLER GSTIN" Then
    MsgBox "Seems, Invoice/s Data for Creating JSON File is not correct or complete. If so, then correct JSON file won't be created. If so, then please first Run Macro for creating Invoice Data - CREATE_INV_DATA_FOR_JSON_EINVOICE_SAMPLE_GIVEN"
    End If
    While (Workbooks("PLAY WITH EXCEL.xlsm").Worksheets("Sheet1").Range("Z" & I).VALUE <> "" Or
```

```
Workbooks("PLAY WITH EXCEL.xlsm").Worksheets("Sheet1").Range("Z" & I + 1).VALUE <> "")
    I = I + 1
    Wend
    I = I + 1
    Workbooks("PLAY WITH EXCEL.xlsm").Worksheets("Sheet1").Range("A" & I & ":AZ50000").VALUE = ""
    Workbooks("PLAY WITH EXCEL.xlsm").Worksheets("Sheet1").Range("A" & I).VALUE = "Below is the JSON Format of the Invoice/s. The same has been written in to " & ActiveWorkbook.Path & "\SAMPLE_JSON_FILE_FOR_EINVOICE.JSON File."
    I = I + 1
    Workbooks("PLAY WITH EXCEL.xlsm").Worksheets("Sheet1").Range("A" & I).VALUE = "["
    II = I + 1
    J = 2
    k = 2
    While ((Workbooks("PLAY WITH EXCEL.xlsm").Worksheets("Sheet1").Range("Z" & J).VALUE <> "" Or Workbooks("PLAY WITH EXCEL.xlsm").Worksheets("Sheet1").Range("Z" & J + 1).VALUE <> "") And II < 50000)
    Workbooks("PLAY WITH EXCEL.xlsm").Worksheets("Sheet1").Range("A" & II).VALUE = "{"
    II = II + 1
    Workbooks("PLAY WITH EXCEL.xlsm").Worksheets("Sheet1").Range("A" & II).VALUE = """" & "Version" & """" & ":" & """" & "1.1" & """" & ","
    II = II + 1
    Workbooks("PLAY WITH EXCEL.xlsm").Worksheets("Sheet1").Range("A" & II).VALUE = """" & "TranDtls" & """" & ":{"
    II = II + 1
    Workbooks("PLAY WITH EXCEL.xlsm").Worksheets("Sheet1").Range("A" & II).VALUE = """" & "TaxSch" & """" & ":" & """" & "GST" & """" & ","
    II = II + 1
    Workbooks("PLAY WITH EXCEL.xlsm").Worksheets("Sheet1").Range("A" & II).VALUE = """" & "SupTyp" & """" & ":" & """" & "B2B" & """" & ","
    II = II + 1
    Workbooks("PLAY WITH EXCEL.xlsm").Worksheets("Sheet1").Range("A" & II).VALUE = """" & "IgstOnIntra" & """" & ":" & """" & "N" & """" & ","
```

```
II = II + 1
Workbooks("PLAY WITH EXCEL.xlsm").Worksheets("Sheet1").Range("A" & II).VALUE = """" & "RegRev" & """" & ":null,"
II = II + 1
Workbooks("PLAY WITH EXCEL.xlsm").Worksheets("Sheet1").Range("A" & II).VALUE = """" & "EcmGstin" & """" & ":null"
II = II + 1
Workbooks("PLAY WITH EXCEL.xlsm").Worksheets("Sheet1").Range("A" & II).VALUE = "},"
II = II + 1
Workbooks("PLAY WITH EXCEL.xlsm").Worksheets("Sheet1").Range("A" & II).VALUE = """" & "DocDtls" & """" & ":{"
II = II + 1
Workbooks("PLAY WITH EXCEL.xlsm").Worksheets("Sheet1").Range("A" & II).VALUE = """" & "Typ" & """" & ":" & """" & "INV" & """" & ","
II = II + 1
Workbooks("PLAY WITH EXCEL.xlsm").Worksheets("Sheet1").Range("A" & II).VALUE = """" & "No" & """" & ":" & """" & Workbooks("PLAY WITH EXCEL.xlsm").Worksheets("Sheet1").Range("A" & J).VALUE & """" & ","
D = Trim(Str(Day(Workbooks("PLAY WITH EXCEL.xlsm").Worksheets("Sheet1").Range("B" & J).VALUE)))
M = Trim(Str(Month(Workbooks("PLAY WITH EXCEL.xlsm").Worksheets("Sheet1").Range("B" & J).VALUE)))
Y = Trim(Str(Year(Workbooks("PLAY WITH EXCEL.xlsm").Worksheets("Sheet1").Range("B" & J).VALUE)))
If Len(D) < 2 Then D = "0" & D
If Len(M) < 2 Then M = "0" & M
II = II + 1
Workbooks("PLAY WITH EXCEL.xlsm").Worksheets("Sheet1").Range("A" & II).VALUE = """" & "Dt" & """" & ":" & """" & D & "/" & M & "/" & Y & """"
II = II + 1
Workbooks("PLAY WITH EXCEL.xlsm").Worksheets("Sheet1").Range("A" & II).VALUE = "},"
'Seller Details
II = II + 1
Workbooks("PLAY WITH EXCEL.xlsm").Worksheets("Sheet1").Range("A" & II).VALUE = """" & "SellerDtls" & """" & ":{"
II = II + 1
```

```
Workbooks("PLAY WITH EXCEL.xlsm").Worksheets("Sheet1").Range("A" & II).VALUE = """" & "Gstin" & """" & ":" & """" & Workbooks("PLAY WITH EXCEL.xlsm").Worksheets("Sheet1").Range("C" & J).VALUE & """" & ","
II = II + 1
Workbooks("PLAY WITH EXCEL.xlsm").Worksheets("Sheet1").Range("A" & II).VALUE = """" & "LglNm" & """" & ":" & """" & Workbooks("PLAY WITH EXCEL.xlsm").Worksheets("Sheet1").Range("D" & J).VALUE & """" & ","
II = II + 1
Workbooks("PLAY WITH EXCEL.xlsm").Worksheets("Sheet1").Range("A" & II).VALUE = """" & "TrdNm" & """" & ":" & "null,"
II = II + 1
Workbooks("PLAY WITH EXCEL.xlsm").Worksheets("Sheet1").Range("A" & II).VALUE = """" & "Addr1" & """" & ":" & """" & Workbooks("PLAY WITH EXCEL.xlsm").Worksheets("Sheet1").Range("E" & J).VALUE & """" & ","
II = II + 1
If Workbooks("PLAY WITH EXCEL.xlsm").Worksheets("Sheet1").Range("F" & J).VALUE = "" Then
Workbooks("PLAY WITH EXCEL.xlsm").Worksheets("Sheet1").Range("A" & II).VALUE = """" & "Addr2" & """" & ":null,"
Else
Workbooks("PLAY WITH EXCEL.xlsm").Worksheets("Sheet1").Range("A" & II).VALUE = """" & "Addr2" & """" & ":" & """" & Workbooks("PLAY WITH EXCEL.xlsm").Worksheets("Sheet1").Range("F" & J).VALUE & """" & ","
End If
II = II + 1
Workbooks("PLAY WITH EXCEL.xlsm").Worksheets("Sheet1").Range("A" & II).VALUE = """" & "Loc" & """" & ":" & """" & Workbooks("PLAY WITH EXCEL.xlsm").Worksheets("Sheet1").Range("G" & J).VALUE & """" & ","
II = II + 1
Workbooks("PLAY WITH EXCEL.xlsm").Worksheets("Sheet1").Range("A" & II).VALUE = """" & "Pin" & """" & ":" & Workbooks("PLAY WITH EXCEL.xlsm").Worksheets("Sheet1").Range("H" & J).VALUE & ","
II = II + 1
Workbooks("PLAY WITH EXCEL.xlsm").Worksheets("Sheet1").Range("A" & II).VALUE = """" & "Stcd" & """" & ":" & """" & Workbooks("PLAY WITH EXCEL.xlsm").Worksheets("Sheet1").Range("I" & J).VALUE & """" & ","
II = II + 1
```

```
Workbooks("PLAY WITH EXCEL.xlsm").Worksheets("Sheet1").Range("A" & II).VALUE = """" & "Ph" & """" & ":null,"
II = II + 1
Workbooks("PLAY WITH EXCEL.xlsm").Worksheets("Sheet1").Range("A" & II).VALUE = """" & "Em" & """" & ":null"
II = II + 1
Workbooks("PLAY WITH EXCEL.xlsm").Worksheets("Sheet1").Range("A" & II).VALUE = "},"
'Buyer Details
II = II + 1
Workbooks("PLAY WITH EXCEL.xlsm").Worksheets("Sheet1").Range("A" & II).VALUE = """" & "BuyerDtls" & """" & ":{"
II = II + 1
Workbooks("PLAY WITH EXCEL.xlsm").Worksheets("Sheet1").Range("A" & II).VALUE = """" & "Gstin" & """" & ":" & """" & Workbooks("PLAY WITH EXCEL.xlsm").Worksheets("Sheet1").Range("J" & J).VALUE & """" & ","
II = II + 1
Workbooks("PLAY WITH EXCEL.xlsm").Worksheets("Sheet1").Range("A" & II).VALUE = """" & "LglNm" & """" & ":" & """" & Workbooks("PLAY WITH EXCEL.xlsm").Worksheets("Sheet1").Range("K" & J).VALUE & """" & ","
II = II + 1
Workbooks("PLAY WITH EXCEL.xlsm").Worksheets("Sheet1").Range("A" & II).VALUE = """" & "TrdNm" & """" & ":" & "null,"
II = II + 1
Workbooks("PLAY WITH EXCEL.xlsm").Worksheets("Sheet1").Range("A" & II).VALUE = """" & "Pos" & """" & ":" & """" & Workbooks("PLAY WITH EXCEL.xlsm").Worksheets("Sheet1").Range("L" & J).VALUE & """" & ","
II = II + 1
Workbooks("PLAY WITH EXCEL.xlsm").Worksheets("Sheet1").Range("A" & II).VALUE = """" & "Addr1" & """" & ":" & """" & Workbooks("PLAY WITH EXCEL.xlsm").Worksheets("Sheet1").Range("M" & J).VALUE & """" & ","
II = II + 1
If Workbooks("PLAY WITH EXCEL.xlsm").Worksheets("Sheet1").Range("N" & J).VALUE = "" Then
Workbooks("PLAY WITH EXCEL.xlsm").Worksheets("Sheet1").Range("A" & II).VALUE = """" & "Addr2" & """" & ":null,"
Else
```

```
Workbooks("PLAY WITH EXCEL.xlsm").Worksheets("Sheet1").Range("A" & II).VALUE = """" & "Addr2" & """" & ":" & """" & Workbooks("PLAY WITH EXCEL.xlsm").Worksheets("Sheet1").Range("N" & J).VALUE & """" & ","
End If
II = II + 1
Workbooks("PLAY WITH EXCEL.xlsm").Worksheets("Sheet1").Range("A" & II).VALUE = """" & "Loc" & """" & ":" & """" & Workbooks("PLAY WITH EXCEL.xlsm").Worksheets("Sheet1").Range("O" & J).VALUE & """" & ","
II = II + 1
Workbooks("PLAY WITH EXCEL.xlsm").Worksheets("Sheet1").Range("A" & II).VALUE = """" & "Pin" & """" & ":" & Workbooks("PLAY WITH EXCEL.xlsm").Worksheets("Sheet1").Range("P" & J).VALUE & ","
II = II + 1
Workbooks("PLAY WITH EXCEL.xlsm").Worksheets("Sheet1").Range("A" & II).VALUE = """" & "Stcd" & """" & ":" & """" & Workbooks("PLAY WITH EXCEL.xlsm").Worksheets("Sheet1").Range("Q" & J).VALUE & """" & ","
II = II + 1
Workbooks("PLAY WITH EXCEL.xlsm").Worksheets("Sheet1").Range("A" & II).VALUE = """" & "Ph" & """" & ":null,"
II = II + 1
Workbooks("PLAY WITH EXCEL.xlsm").Worksheets("Sheet1").Range("A" & II).VALUE = """" & "Em" & """" & ":null"
II = II + 1
Workbooks("PLAY WITH EXCEL.xlsm").Worksheets("Sheet1").Range("A" & II).VALUE = "},"
'Ship-to-Details
If UCase(Workbooks("PLAY WITH EXCEL.xlsm").Worksheets("Sheet1").Range("AU" & J).VALUE) <> "Y" And UCase(Workbooks("PLAY WITH EXCEL.xlsm").Worksheets("Sheet1").Range("AU" & J).VALUE) <> "YES" Then
II = II + 1
Workbooks("PLAY WITH EXCEL.xlsm").Worksheets("Sheet1").Range("A" & II).VALUE = """" & "ShipDtls" & """" & ":null,"
Else
II = II + 1
Workbooks("PLAY WITH EXCEL.xlsm").Worksheets("Sheet1").Range("A" & II).VALUE = """" & "ShipDtls" & """" & ":{"
II = II + 1
```

```
Workbooks("PLAY WITH EXCEL.xlsm").Worksheets("Sheet1").Range("A" & II).VALUE = """" & "Gstin" & """" & ":" & """" & Workbooks("PLAY WITH EXCEL.xlsm").Worksheets("Sheet1").Range("R" & J).VALUE & """" & ","
II = II + 1
Workbooks("PLAY WITH EXCEL.xlsm").Worksheets("Sheet1").Range("A" & II).VALUE = """" & "LglNm" & """" & ":" & """" & Workbooks("PLAY WITH EXCEL.xlsm").Worksheets("Sheet1").Range("S" & J).VALUE & """" & ","
II = II + 1
Workbooks("PLAY WITH EXCEL.xlsm").Worksheets("Sheet1").Range("A" & II).VALUE = """" & "TrdNm" & """" & ":" & "null,"
II = II + 1
Workbooks("PLAY WITH EXCEL.xlsm").Worksheets("Sheet1").Range("A" & II).VALUE = """" & "Addr1" & """" & ":" & """" & Workbooks("PLAY WITH EXCEL.xlsm").Worksheets("Sheet1").Range("T" & J).VALUE & """" & ","
II = II + 1
If Workbooks("PLAY WITH EXCEL.xlsm").Worksheets("Sheet1").Range("U" & J).VALUE = "" Then
Workbooks("PLAY WITH EXCEL.xlsm").Worksheets("Sheet1").Range("A" & II).VALUE = """" & "Addr2" & """" & ":null,"
Else
Workbooks("PLAY WITH EXCEL.xlsm").Worksheets("Sheet1").Range("A" & II).VALUE = """" & "Addr2" & """" & ":" & """" & Workbooks("PLAY WITH EXCEL.xlsm").Worksheets("Sheet1").Range("U" & J).VALUE & """" & ","
End If
II = II + 1
Workbooks("PLAY WITH EXCEL.xlsm").Worksheets("Sheet1").Range("A" & II).VALUE = """" & "Loc" & """" & ":" & """" & Workbooks("PLAY WITH EXCEL.xlsm").Worksheets("Sheet1").Range("V" & J).VALUE & """" & ","
II = II + 1
Workbooks("PLAY WITH EXCEL.xlsm").Worksheets("Sheet1").Range("A" & II).VALUE = """" & "Pin" & """" & ":" & Workbooks("PLAY WITH EXCEL.xlsm").Worksheets("Sheet1").Range("W" & J).VALUE & ","
II = II + 1
Workbooks("PLAY WITH EXCEL.xlsm").Worksheets("Sheet1").Range("A" & II).VALUE = """" & "Stcd" & """" & ":" & """" & Workbooks("PLAY WITH EXCEL.xlsm").Worksheets("Sheet1").Range("X" & J).VALUE & """"
II = II + 1
```

```
Workbooks("PLAY WITH EXCEL.xlsm").Worksheets("Sheet1").Range("A" & II).VALUE = "},"
End If
'Value Details
II = II + 1
Workbooks("PLAY WITH EXCEL.xlsm").Worksheets("Sheet1").Range("A" & II).VALUE = """" & "ValDtls" & """" & ":{"
If Workbooks("PLAY WITH EXCEL.xlsm").Worksheets("Sheet1").Range("AB" & J).VALUE = "" Then Workbooks("PLAY WITH EXCEL.xlsm").Worksheets("Sheet1").Range("AB" & J).VALUE = 0
If Workbooks("PLAY WITH EXCEL.xlsm").Worksheets("Sheet1").Range("AD" & J).VALUE = "" Then Workbooks("PLAY WITH EXCEL.xlsm").Worksheets("Sheet1").Range("AD" & J).VALUE = 0
If Workbooks("PLAY WITH EXCEL.xlsm").Worksheets("Sheet1").Range("AE" & J).VALUE = "" Then Workbooks("PLAY WITH EXCEL.xlsm").Worksheets("Sheet1").Range("AE" & J).VALUE = 0
If Workbooks("PLAY WITH EXCEL.xlsm").Worksheets("Sheet1").Range("AG" & J).VALUE = "" Then Workbooks("PLAY WITH EXCEL.xlsm").Worksheets("Sheet1").Range("AG" & J).VALUE = "0%"
If Workbooks("PLAY WITH EXCEL.xlsm").Worksheets("Sheet1").Range("AH" & J).VALUE = "" Then Workbooks("PLAY WITH EXCEL.xlsm").Worksheets("Sheet1").Range("AH" & J).VALUE = "0%"
If Workbooks("PLAY WITH EXCEL.xlsm").Worksheets("Sheet1").Range("AI" & J).VALUE = "" Then Workbooks("PLAY WITH EXCEL.xlsm").Worksheets("Sheet1").Range("AI" & J).VALUE = "0%"
If Workbooks("PLAY WITH EXCEL.xlsm").Worksheets("Sheet1").Range("AK" & J).VALUE = "" Then Workbooks("PLAY WITH EXCEL.xlsm").Worksheets("Sheet1").Range("AK" & J).VALUE = 0
If Workbooks("PLAY WITH EXCEL.xlsm").Worksheets("Sheet1").Range("AL" & J).VALUE = "" Then Workbooks("PLAY WITH EXCEL.xlsm").Worksheets("Sheet1").Range("AL" &
```

```
J).VALUE = 0
    k = J
    ASSVAL = 0
    IGST = 0
    CGST = 0
    SGST = 0
    While (Workbooks("PLAY WITH EXCEL.xlsm").Worksheets("Sheet1").Range("AC" & k).VALUE <> "")
    ASSVAL = ASSVAL + Round((Workbooks("PLAY WITH EXCEL.xlsm").Worksheets("Sheet1").Range("AA" & k).VALUE - Workbooks("PLAY WITH EXCEL.xlsm").Worksheets("Sheet1").Range("AB" & k).VALUE) * Workbooks("PLAY WITH EXCEL.xlsm").Worksheets("Sheet1").Range("AD" & k).VALUE, 2)
    IGST = IGST + Round(((Workbooks("PLAY WITH EXCEL.xlsm").Worksheets("Sheet1").Range("AA" & k).VALUE - Workbooks("PLAY WITH EXCEL.xlsm").Worksheets("Sheet1").Range("AB" & k).VALUE) * Workbooks("PLAY WITH EXCEL.xlsm").Worksheets("Sheet1").Range("AD" & k).VALUE) * Workbooks("PLAY WITH EXCEL.xlsm").Worksheets("Sheet1").Range("AG" & k).VALUE, 2)
    CGST = CGST + Round(((Workbooks("PLAY WITH EXCEL.xlsm").Worksheets("Sheet1").Range("AA" & k).VALUE - Workbooks("PLAY WITH EXCEL.xlsm").Worksheets("Sheet1").Range("AB" & k).VALUE) * Workbooks("PLAY WITH EXCEL.xlsm").Worksheets("Sheet1").Range("AD" & k).VALUE) * Workbooks("PLAY WITH EXCEL.xlsm").Worksheets("Sheet1").Range("AH" & k).VALUE, 2)
    SGST = SGST + Round(((Workbooks("PLAY WITH EXCEL.xlsm").Worksheets("Sheet1").Range("AA" & k).VALUE - Workbooks("PLAY WITH EXCEL.xlsm").Worksheets("Sheet1").Range("AB" & k).VALUE) * Workbooks("PLAY WITH EXCEL.xlsm").Worksheets("Sheet1").Range("AD" & k).VALUE) * Workbooks("PLAY WITH EXCEL.xlsm").Worksheets("Sheet1").Range("AI" & k).VALUE, 2)
    k = k + 1
    Wend
    ASSVAL = Round(ASSVAL, 2)
    IGST = Round(IGST, 2)
```

```
CGST = Round(CGST, 2)
SGST = Round(SGST, 2)
II = II + 1
Workbooks("PLAY WITH EXCEL.xlsm").Worksheets("Sheet1").Range("A" & II).VALUE = """" & "AssVal" & """" & ":" & ASSVAL & ","
II = II + 1
Workbooks("PLAY WITH EXCEL.xlsm").Worksheets("Sheet1").Range("A" & II).VALUE = """" & "IgstVal" & """" & ":" & IGST & ","
II = II + 1
Workbooks("PLAY WITH EXCEL.xlsm").Worksheets("Sheet1").Range("A" & II).VALUE = """" & "CgstVal" & """" & ":" & CGST & ","
II = II + 1
Workbooks("PLAY WITH EXCEL.xlsm").Worksheets("Sheet1").Range("A" & II).VALUE = """" & "SgstVal" & """" & ":" & SGST & ","
II = II + 1
Workbooks("PLAY WITH EXCEL.xlsm").Worksheets("Sheet1").Range("A" & II).VALUE = """" & "CesVal" & """" & ":0,"
II = II + 1
Workbooks("PLAY WITH EXCEL.xlsm").Worksheets("Sheet1").Range("A" & II).VALUE = """" & "StCesVal" & """" & ":0,"
II = II + 1
Workbooks("PLAY WITH EXCEL.xlsm").Worksheets("Sheet1").Range("A" & II).VALUE = """" & "Discount" & """" & ":0,"
II = II + 1
Workbooks("PLAY WITH EXCEL.xlsm").Worksheets("Sheet1").Range("A" & II).VALUE = """" & "OthChrg" & """" & ":" & Workbooks("PLAY WITH EXCEL.xlsm").Worksheets("Sheet1").Range("AK" & J).VALUE & ","
II = II + 1
Workbooks("PLAY WITH EXCEL.xlsm").Worksheets("Sheet1").Range("A" & II).VALUE = """" & "RndOffAmt" & """" & ":" & Workbooks("PLAY WITH EXCEL.xlsm").Worksheets("Sheet1").Range("AL" & J).VALUE & ","
II = II + 1
Workbooks("PLAY WITH EXCEL.xlsm").Worksheets("Sheet1").Range("A" & II).VALUE = """" & "TotInvVal" & """" & ":" & Round(ASSVAL + IGST + SGST + CGST + Workbooks("PLAY WITH EXCEL.xlsm").Worksheets("Sheet1").Range("AK" & J).VALUE + Workbooks("PLAY WITH EXCEL.xlsm").Worksheets("Sheet1").Range("AL" & J).VALUE, 0)
```

```
    II = II + 1
    Workbooks("PLAY WITH EXCEL.xlsm").Worksheets("Sheet1").Range("A" &
II).VALUE = "},"
    II = II + 1
    Workbooks("PLAY WITH EXCEL.xlsm").Worksheets("Sheet1").Range("A" &
II).VALUE = """" & "ExpDtls" & """" & ":{"
    II = II + 1
    Workbooks("PLAY WITH EXCEL.xlsm").Worksheets("Sheet1").Range("A" &
II).VALUE = """" & "ShipBNo" & """" & ":null,"
    II = II + 1
    Workbooks("PLAY WITH EXCEL.xlsm").Worksheets("Sheet1").Range("A" &
II).VALUE = """" & "ShipBDt" & """" & ":null,"
    II = II + 1
    Workbooks("PLAY WITH EXCEL.xlsm").Worksheets("Sheet1").Range("A" &
II).VALUE = """" & "Port" & """" & ":null,"
    II = II + 1
    Workbooks("PLAY WITH EXCEL.xlsm").Worksheets("Sheet1").Range("A" &
II).VALUE = """" & "RefClm" & """" & ":null,"
    II = II + 1
    Workbooks("PLAY WITH EXCEL.xlsm").Worksheets("Sheet1").Range("A" &
II).VALUE = """" & "ForCur" & """" & ":null,"
    II = II + 1
    Workbooks("PLAY WITH EXCEL.xlsm").Worksheets("Sheet1").Range("A" &
II).VALUE = """" & "CntCode" & """" & ":null,"
    II = II + 1
    Workbooks("PLAY WITH EXCEL.xlsm").Worksheets("Sheet1").Range("A" &
II).VALUE = """" & "ExpDuty" & """" & ":0"
    II = II + 1
    Workbooks("PLAY WITH EXCEL.xlsm").Worksheets("Sheet1").Range("A" &
II).VALUE = "},"
    'EWAYBILL DETAILS
    If UCase(Workbooks("PLAY WITH
EXCEL.xlsm").Worksheets("Sheet1").Range("AV" & J).VALUE) = "Y" Or
UCase(Workbooks("PLAY WITH
EXCEL.xlsm").Worksheets("Sheet1").Range("AV" & J).VALUE) = "YES" Then
    II = II + 1
    Workbooks("PLAY WITH EXCEL.xlsm").Worksheets("Sheet1").Range("A" &
II).VALUE = """" & "EwbDtls" & """" & ":{"
```

```
II = II + 1
If Workbooks("PLAY WITH EXCEL.xlsm").Worksheets("Sheet1").Range("AM" & J).VALUE = "" Then
Workbooks("PLAY WITH EXCEL.xlsm").Worksheets("Sheet1").Range("A" & II).VALUE = """" & "TransId" & """" & ":null,"
Else
Workbooks("PLAY WITH EXCEL.xlsm").Worksheets("Sheet1").Range("A" & II).VALUE = """" & "TransId" & """" & ":" & """" & Workbooks("PLAY WITH EXCEL.xlsm").Worksheets("Sheet1").Range("AM" & J).VALUE & """" & ","
End If
II = II + 1
If Workbooks("PLAY WITH EXCEL.xlsm").Worksheets("Sheet1").Range("AN" & J).VALUE = "" Then
Workbooks("PLAY WITH EXCEL.xlsm").Worksheets("Sheet1").Range("A" & II).VALUE = """" & "TransName" & """" & ":null,"
Else
Workbooks("PLAY WITH EXCEL.xlsm").Worksheets("Sheet1").Range("A" & II).VALUE = """" & "TransName" & """" & ":" & """" & Workbooks("PLAY WITH EXCEL.xlsm").Worksheets("Sheet1").Range("AN" & J).VALUE & """" & ","
End If
II = II + 1
Workbooks("PLAY WITH EXCEL.xlsm").Worksheets("Sheet1").Range("A" & II).VALUE = """" & "TransMode" & """" & ":" & """" & Workbooks("PLAY WITH EXCEL.xlsm").Worksheets("Sheet1").Range("AO" & J).VALUE & """" & ","
II = II + 1
Workbooks("PLAY WITH EXCEL.xlsm").Worksheets("Sheet1").Range("A" & II).VALUE = """" & "Distance" & """" & ":" & Workbooks("PLAY WITH EXCEL.xlsm").Worksheets("Sheet1").Range("AP" & J).VALUE & ","
II = II + 1
If Workbooks("PLAY WITH EXCEL.xlsm").Worksheets("Sheet1").Range("AQ" & J).VALUE = "" Then
Workbooks("PLAY WITH EXCEL.xlsm").Worksheets("Sheet1").Range("A" & II).VALUE = """" & "TransDocNo" & """" & ":null,"
Else
Workbooks("PLAY WITH EXCEL.xlsm").Worksheets("Sheet1").Range("A" & II).VALUE = """" & "TransDocNo" & """" & ":" & """" & Workbooks("PLAY WITH EXCEL.xlsm").Worksheets("Sheet1").Range("AQ" & J).VALUE & """" & ","
End If
```

```
If IsDate(Workbooks("PLAY WITH EXCEL.xlsm").Worksheets("Sheet1").Range("AR" & J).VALUE) = True Then
D = Trim(Str(Day(Workbooks("PLAY WITH EXCEL.xlsm").Worksheets("Sheet1").Range("AR" & J).VALUE)))
M = Trim(Str(Month(Workbooks("PLAY WITH EXCEL.xlsm").Worksheets("Sheet1").Range("AR" & J).VALUE)))
Y = Trim(Str(Year(Workbooks("PLAY WITH EXCEL.xlsm").Worksheets("Sheet1").Range("AR" & J).VALUE)))
If Len(D) < 2 Then D = "0" & D
If Len(M) < 2 Then M = "0" & M
II = II + 1
Workbooks("PLAY WITH EXCEL.xlsm").Worksheets("Sheet1").Range("A" & II).VALUE = """" & "TransDocDt" & """" & ":" & """" & D & "/" & M & "/" & Y & """" & ","
Else
II = II + 1
Workbooks("PLAY WITH EXCEL.xlsm").Worksheets("Sheet1").Range("A" & II).VALUE = """" & "TransDocDt" & """" & ":null,"
End If
II = II + 1
Workbooks("PLAY WITH EXCEL.xlsm").Worksheets("Sheet1").Range("A" & II).VALUE = """" & "VehNo" & """" & ":" & """" & Workbooks("PLAY WITH EXCEL.xlsm").Worksheets("Sheet1").Range("AS" & J).VALUE & """" & ","
II = II + 1
Workbooks("PLAY WITH EXCEL.xlsm").Worksheets("Sheet1").Range("A" & II).VALUE = """" & "VehType" & """" & ":" & """" & Workbooks("PLAY WITH EXCEL.xlsm").Worksheets("Sheet1").Range("AT" & J).VALUE & """"
II = II + 1
Workbooks("PLAY WITH EXCEL.xlsm").Worksheets("Sheet1").Range("A" & II).VALUE = "},"
End If
'RETRIVING ITEMS
SL = 0
While (Workbooks("PLAY WITH EXCEL.xlsm").Worksheets("Sheet1").Range("Z" & J).VALUE <> "")
SL = SL + 1
II = II + 1
```

```
If Workbooks("PLAY WITH EXCEL.xlsm").Worksheets("Sheet1").Range("AB" & J).VALUE = "" Then Workbooks("PLAY WITH EXCEL.xlsm").Worksheets("Sheet1").Range("AB" & J).VALUE = 0
If Workbooks("PLAY WITH EXCEL.xlsm").Worksheets("Sheet1").Range("AD" & J).VALUE = "" Then Workbooks("PLAY WITH EXCEL.xlsm").Worksheets("Sheet1").Range("AD" & J).VALUE = 0
If Workbooks("PLAY WITH EXCEL.xlsm").Worksheets("Sheet1").Range("AE" & J).VALUE = "" Then Workbooks("PLAY WITH EXCEL.xlsm").Worksheets("Sheet1").Range("AE" & J).VALUE = 0
If Workbooks("PLAY WITH EXCEL.xlsm").Worksheets("Sheet1").Range("AG" & J).VALUE = "" Then Workbooks("PLAY WITH EXCEL.xlsm").Worksheets("Sheet1").Range("AG" & J).VALUE = "0%"
If Workbooks("PLAY WITH EXCEL.xlsm").Worksheets("Sheet1").Range("AH" & J).VALUE = "" Then Workbooks("PLAY WITH EXCEL.xlsm").Worksheets("Sheet1").Range("AH" & J).VALUE = "0%"
If Workbooks("PLAY WITH EXCEL.xlsm").Worksheets("Sheet1").Range("AI" & J).VALUE = "" Then Workbooks("PLAY WITH EXCEL.xlsm").Worksheets("Sheet1").Range("AI" & J).VALUE = "0%"
If Workbooks("PLAY WITH EXCEL.xlsm").Worksheets("Sheet1").Range("AK" & J).VALUE = "" Then Workbooks("PLAY WITH EXCEL.xlsm").Worksheets("Sheet1").Range("AK" & J).VALUE = 0
If Workbooks("PLAY WITH EXCEL.xlsm").Worksheets("Sheet1").Range("AL" & J).VALUE = "" Then Workbooks("PLAY WITH EXCEL.xlsm").Worksheets("Sheet1").Range("AL" & J).VALUE = 0
Workbooks("PLAY WITH EXCEL.xlsm").Worksheets("Sheet1").Range("A" & II).VALUE = """" & "ItemList" & """" & ":[{"
If SL > 1 Then Workbooks("PLAY WITH EXCEL.xlsm").Worksheets("Sheet1").Range("A" & II).VALUE = "{"
II = II + 1
```

```
Workbooks("PLAY WITH EXCEL.xlsm").Worksheets("Sheet1").Range("A" & II).VALUE = """" & "SlNo" & """" & ":" & """" & SL & """" & ","
II = II + 1
Workbooks("PLAY WITH EXCEL.xlsm").Worksheets("Sheet1").Range("A" & II).VALUE = """" & "PrdDesc" & """" & ":" & """" & Workbooks("PLAY WITH EXCEL.xlsm").Worksheets("Sheet1").Range("Z" & J).VALUE & """" & ","
II = II + 1
Workbooks("PLAY WITH EXCEL.xlsm").Worksheets("Sheet1").Range("A" & II).VALUE = """" & "IsServc" & """" & ":" & """" & "N" & """" & ","
II = II + 1
Workbooks("PLAY WITH EXCEL.xlsm").Worksheets("Sheet1").Range("A" & II).VALUE = """" & "HsnCd" & """" & ":" & """" & Workbooks("PLAY WITH EXCEL.xlsm").Worksheets("Sheet1").Range("Y" & J).VALUE & """" & ","
II = II + 1
Workbooks("PLAY WITH EXCEL.xlsm").Worksheets("Sheet1").Range("A" & II).VALUE = """" & "Qty" & """" & ":" & Workbooks("PLAY WITH EXCEL.xlsm").Worksheets("Sheet1").Range("AA" & J).VALUE & ","
II = II + 1
If Workbooks("PLAY WITH EXCEL.xlsm").Worksheets("Sheet1").Range("AB" & J).VALUE = "" Then
Workbooks("PLAY WITH EXCEL.xlsm").Worksheets("Sheet1").Range("A" & II).VALUE = """" & "FreeQty" & """" & ":0,"
Else
Workbooks("PLAY WITH EXCEL.xlsm").Worksheets("Sheet1").Range("A" & II).VALUE = """" & "FreeQty" & """" & ":" & Workbooks("PLAY WITH EXCEL.xlsm").Worksheets("Sheet1").Range("AB" & J).VALUE & ","
End If
II = II + 1
Workbooks("PLAY WITH EXCEL.xlsm").Worksheets("Sheet1").Range("A" & II).VALUE = """" & "Unit" & """" & ":" & """" & Workbooks("PLAY WITH EXCEL.xlsm").Worksheets("Sheet1").Range("AC" & J).VALUE & """" & ","
II = II + 1
Workbooks("PLAY WITH EXCEL.xlsm").Worksheets("Sheet1").Range("A" & II).VALUE = """" & "UnitPrice" & """" & ":" & Workbooks("PLAY WITH EXCEL.xlsm").Worksheets("Sheet1").Range("AD" & J).VALUE & ","
II = II + 1
Workbooks("PLAY WITH EXCEL.xlsm").Worksheets("Sheet1").Range("A" & II).VALUE = """" & "TotAmt" & """" & ":" & Round(Workbooks("PLAY WITH
```

```
EXCEL.xlsm").Worksheets("Sheet1").Range("AA" & J).VALUE * Workbooks("PLAY WITH EXCEL.xlsm").Worksheets("Sheet1").Range("AD" & J).VALUE, 2) & ","
    'DISCOUNT
    II = II + 1
    Workbooks("PLAY WITH EXCEL.xlsm").Worksheets("Sheet1").Range("A" & II).VALUE = """" & "Discount" & """" & ":" & Round(Workbooks("PLAY WITH EXCEL.xlsm").Worksheets("Sheet1").Range("AB" & J).VALUE * Workbooks("PLAY WITH EXCEL.xlsm").Worksheets("Sheet1").Range("AD" & J).VALUE, 2) & ","
    II = II + 1
    Workbooks("PLAY WITH EXCEL.xlsm").Worksheets("Sheet1").Range("A" & II).VALUE = """" & "PreTaxVal" & """" & ":0,"
    'ASSAMT
    II = II + 1
    Workbooks("PLAY WITH EXCEL.xlsm").Worksheets("Sheet1").Range("A" & II).VALUE = """" & "AssAmt" & """" & ":" & Round((Workbooks("PLAY WITH EXCEL.xlsm").Worksheets("Sheet1").Range("AA" & J).VALUE - Workbooks("PLAY WITH EXCEL.xlsm").Worksheets("Sheet1").Range("AB" & J).VALUE) * Workbooks("PLAY WITH EXCEL.xlsm").Worksheets("Sheet1").Range("AD" & J).VALUE, 2) & ","
    'GSTRATE
    II = II + 1
    Workbooks("PLAY WITH EXCEL.xlsm").Worksheets("Sheet1").Range("A" & II).VALUE = """" & "GstRt" & """" & ":" & (Workbooks("PLAY WITH EXCEL.xlsm").Worksheets("Sheet1").Range("AG" & J).VALUE + Workbooks("PLAY WITH EXCEL.xlsm").Worksheets("Sheet1").Range("AH" & J).VALUE + Workbooks("PLAY WITH EXCEL.xlsm").Worksheets("Sheet1").Range("AI" & J).VALUE) * 100 & ","
    'IGST
    II = II + 1
    Workbooks("PLAY WITH EXCEL.xlsm").Worksheets("Sheet1").Range("A" & II).VALUE = """" & "IgstAmt" & """" & ":" & Round(Round(((Workbooks("PLAY WITH EXCEL.xlsm").Worksheets("Sheet1").Range("AA" & J).VALUE - Workbooks("PLAY WITH EXCEL.xlsm").Worksheets("Sheet1").Range("AB" & J).VALUE) * Workbooks("PLAY WITH EXCEL.xlsm").Worksheets("Sheet1").Range("AD" & J).VALUE), 2) * Workbooks("PLAY WITH EXCEL.xlsm").Worksheets("Sheet1").Range("AG" &
```

```
J).VALUE, 2) & ","
    'CGST
    II = II + 1
    Workbooks("PLAY WITH EXCEL.xlsm").Worksheets("Sheet1").Range("A" & II).VALUE = """" & "CgstAmt" & """" & ":" & Round(Round(((Workbooks("PLAY WITH EXCEL.xlsm").Worksheets("Sheet1").Range("AA" & J).VALUE - Workbooks("PLAY WITH EXCEL.xlsm").Worksheets("Sheet1").Range("AB" & J).VALUE) * Workbooks("PLAY WITH EXCEL.xlsm").Worksheets("Sheet1").Range("AD" & J).VALUE), 2) * Workbooks("PLAY WITH EXCEL.xlsm").Worksheets("Sheet1").Range("AH" & J).VALUE, 2) & ","
    'SGST
    II = II + 1
    Workbooks("PLAY WITH EXCEL.xlsm").Worksheets("Sheet1").Range("A" & II).VALUE = """" & "SgstAmt" & """" & ":" & Round(Round(((Workbooks("PLAY WITH EXCEL.xlsm").Worksheets("Sheet1").Range("AA" & J).VALUE - Workbooks("PLAY WITH EXCEL.xlsm").Worksheets("Sheet1").Range("AB" & J).VALUE) * Workbooks("PLAY WITH EXCEL.xlsm").Worksheets("Sheet1").Range("AD" & J).VALUE), 2) * Workbooks("PLAY WITH EXCEL.xlsm").Worksheets("Sheet1").Range("AI" & J).VALUE, 2) & ","
    II = II + 1
    Workbooks("PLAY WITH EXCEL.xlsm").Worksheets("Sheet1").Range("A" & II).VALUE = """" & "CesRt" & """" & ":0,"
    II = II + 1
    Workbooks("PLAY WITH EXCEL.xlsm").Worksheets("Sheet1").Range("A" & II).VALUE = """" & "CesAmt" & """" & ":0,"
    II = II + 1
    Workbooks("PLAY WITH EXCEL.xlsm").Worksheets("Sheet1").Range("A" & II).VALUE = """" & "CesNonAdvlAmt" & """" & ":0,"
    II = II + 1
    Workbooks("PLAY WITH EXCEL.xlsm").Worksheets("Sheet1").Range("A" & II).VALUE = """" & "StateCesRt" & """" & ":0,"
    II = II + 1
    Workbooks("PLAY WITH EXCEL.xlsm").Worksheets("Sheet1").Range("A" & II).VALUE = """" & "StateCesAmt" & """" & ":0,"
    II = II + 1
```

Workbooks("PLAY WITH EXCEL.xlsm").Worksheets("Sheet1").Range("A" & II).VALUE = """" & "StateCesNonAdvlAmt" & """" & ":0,"

II = II + 1

Workbooks("PLAY WITH EXCEL.xlsm").Worksheets("Sheet1").Range("A" & II).VALUE = """" & "OthChrg" & """" & ":0,"

II = II + 1

'TOTITEMVAL

Dim VALUE As Double

VALUE = 0

VALUE = ((Workbooks("PLAY WITH EXCEL.xlsm").Worksheets("Sheet1").Range("AA" & J).VALUE - Workbooks("PLAY WITH EXCEL.xlsm").Worksheets("Sheet1").Range("AB" & J).VALUE) * Workbooks("PLAY WITH EXCEL.xlsm").Worksheets("Sheet1").Range("AD" & J).VALUE)

VALUE = VALUE + ((Workbooks("PLAY WITH EXCEL.xlsm").Worksheets("Sheet1").Range("AA" & J).VALUE - Workbooks("PLAY WITH EXCEL.xlsm").Worksheets("Sheet1").Range("AB" & J).VALUE) * Workbooks("PLAY WITH EXCEL.xlsm").Worksheets("Sheet1").Range("AD" & J).VALUE) * Workbooks("PLAY WITH EXCEL.xlsm").Worksheets("Sheet1").Range("AG" & J).VALUE

VALUE = VALUE + ((Workbooks("PLAY WITH EXCEL.xlsm").Worksheets("Sheet1").Range("AA" & J).VALUE - Workbooks("PLAY WITH EXCEL.xlsm").Worksheets("Sheet1").Range("AB" & J).VALUE) * Workbooks("PLAY WITH EXCEL.xlsm").Worksheets("Sheet1").Range("AD" & J).VALUE) * Workbooks("PLAY WITH EXCEL.xlsm").Worksheets("Sheet1").Range("AH" & J).VALUE

VALUE = VALUE + ((Workbooks("PLAY WITH EXCEL.xlsm").Worksheets("Sheet1").Range("AA" & J).VALUE - Workbooks("PLAY WITH EXCEL.xlsm").Worksheets("Sheet1").Range("AB" & J).VALUE) * Workbooks("PLAY WITH EXCEL.xlsm").Worksheets("Sheet1").Range("AD" & J).VALUE) * Workbooks("PLAY WITH EXCEL.xlsm").Worksheets("Sheet1").Range("AI" & J).VALUE

VALUE = Round(VALUE, 2)

Workbooks("PLAY WITH EXCEL.xlsm").Worksheets("Sheet1").Range("A" & II).VALUE = """" & "TotItemVal" & """" & ":" & VALUE

```
'ActiveSheet.Range("A" & II).VALUE = """" & "TotItemVal" & """" & ":" & Round(((ActiveSheet.Range("AA" & J).VALUE - ActiveSheet.Range("AB" & J).VALUE) * ActiveSheet.Range("AD" & J).VALUE) + ((ActiveSheet.Range("AA" & J).VALUE - ActiveSheet.Range("AB" & J).VALUE) * ActiveSheet.Range("AD" & J).VALUE) * ActiveSheet.Range("AG" & J).VALUE + ((ActiveSheet.Range("AA" & J).VALUE - ActiveSheet.Range("AB" & J).VALUE) * ActiveSheet.Range("AD" & J).VALUE) * ActiveSheet.Range("AH" & J).VALUE + ((ActiveSheet.Range("AA" & J).VALUE - ActiveSheet.Range("AB" & J).VALUE) * ActiveSheet.Range("AD" & J).VALUE) * ActiveSheet.Range("AI" & J).VALUE, 2)
II = II + 1
Workbooks("PLAY WITH EXCEL.xlsm").Worksheets("Sheet1").Range("A" & II).VALUE = "},"
J = J + 1
Wend
Workbooks("PLAY WITH EXCEL.xlsm").Worksheets("Sheet1").Range("A" & II).VALUE = Left(Workbooks("PLAY WITH EXCEL.xlsm").Worksheets("Sheet1").Range("A" & II).VALUE, Len(Workbooks("PLAY WITH EXCEL.xlsm").Worksheets("Sheet1").Range("A" & II).VALUE) - 1)
II = II + 1
Workbooks("PLAY WITH EXCEL.xlsm").Worksheets("Sheet1").Range("A" & II).VALUE = "]"
II = II + 1
Workbooks("PLAY WITH EXCEL.xlsm").Worksheets("Sheet1").Range("A" & II).VALUE = "},"
II = II + 1
J = J + 1
Wend
II = II - 1
Workbooks("PLAY WITH EXCEL.xlsm").Worksheets("Sheet1").Range("A" & II).VALUE = "}"
II = II + 1
Workbooks("PLAY WITH EXCEL.xlsm").Worksheets("Sheet1").Range("A" & II).VALUE = "]"
'creating json file
Dim S1 As String
S1 = ActiveWorkbook.Path & "\SAMPLE_JSON_FILE_FOR_EINVOICE.JSON"
```

```
S2 = Dir(S1)
If S2 <> "" Then
J = MsgBox("The File (" & S1 & ") already exists. Click YES to replace that file with new data?", vbYesNo)
If J = 6 Then
Kill (S1)
Else
MsgBox ("FOR CREATING JSON FILE, YOU HAVE TO DELETE EXISTING JSON FILE - " & S1)
Exit Sub
End If
End If
Set fs = CreateObject("Scripting.FileSystemObject")
Set A = fs.CreateTextFile(S1)
While (Workbooks("PLAY WITH EXCEL.xlsm").Worksheets("Sheet1").Range("A" & I).VALUE <> "")
A.WriteLine (Workbooks("PLAY WITH EXCEL.xlsm").Worksheets("Sheet1").Range("A" & I).VALUE)
I = I + 1
Wend
A.Close
MsgBox ("JSON FILE for EInvoicing has been created. Find it here : " & S1)
Exit Sub
ERR:
MsgBox ERR.Number & " " & ERR.Description
End Sub
```

21

Find Prime Numbers

Sub Find_Prime_Numbers()

```
On Error GoTo ERR
    Dim I, J, N1, N2 As Long
    Dim P, TOTPRIME As Long
    Dim N3 As Integer
    Workbooks("PLAY WITH EXCEL.xlsm").Worksheets("Sheet1").Activate
    Workbooks("PLAY WITH EXCEL.xlsm").Worksheets("Sheet1").Range("A1").Select
    P = 0
    TOTPRIME = 0
    N3 = 0
    N1 = InputBox("ENTER START NUMBER")
    N2 = InputBox("ENTER END NUMBER")
    If N2 < N1 Then
    I = N1
    N1 = N2
    N2 = I
    End If
    If N1 < 2 Then N1 = 2
    C = 65
    r = 2
    J = 0
    Workbooks("PLAY WITH EXCEL.xlsm").Worksheets("Sheet1").Range("A1:Z5000").VALUE = ""
```

```
Workbooks("PLAY WITH EXCEL.xlsm").Worksheets("Sheet1").Range("A1:Z5000").Select
Selection.NumberFormat = "General"
Workbooks("PLAY WITH EXCEL.xlsm").Worksheets("Sheet1").Range("A1").Select
Workbooks("PLAY WITH EXCEL.xlsm").Worksheets("Sheet1").Range("A1").VALUE = "ALL PRIME NUMBERS BETWEEN " & N1 & " AND " & N2 & " :"
For I = N1 To N2
If I < 11 Then
For J = 2 To I
If I / J = Int(I / J) Then P = P + 1
Next J
If P = 1 Then
TOTPRIME = TOTPRIME + 1
Workbooks("PLAY WITH EXCEL.xlsm").Worksheets("Sheet1").Range(Chr(C) & r).VALUE = I
If C > 75 Then
C = 65
r = r + 1
Else
C = C + 1
End If
End If
P = 0
Else
If I / 2 = Int(I / 2) Or I / 3 = Int(I / 3) Or I / 5 = Int(I / 5) Or I / 7 = Int(I / 7) Then
P = P + 1
Else
J = 11
For J = 11 To I / J Step 2
If J / 3 <> Int(J / 3) And J / 5 <> Int(J / 5) And J / 7 <> Int(J / 7) Then
If I / J = Int(I / J) Then
P = P + 1
Exit For
End If
End If
```

```
Next J
End If
If P = 0 Then
TOTPRIME = TOTPRIME + 1
Workbooks("PLAY                                                    WITH
EXCEL.xlsm").Worksheets("Sheet1").Range(Chr(C) & r).VALUE = I
If C > 75 Then
C = 65
r = r + 1
Workbooks("PLAY                                                    WITH
EXCEL.xlsm").Worksheets("Sheet1").Range(Chr(C) & r).Select
Else
C = C + 1
End If
End If
P = 0
End If
If (I / 50000 = Int(I / 50000)) And ((N2 - I) > 10000) Then
N3 = MsgBox("Found Prime Numbers up to " & I & "--- Have to find Primer
Numbers up to " & N2 & "--- It may take long. Click on YES to stop now or
Cancel to continue.", vbYesNo)
If N3 = 6 Then
N2 = I
Exit For
End If
End If
Next I
Workbooks("PLAY WITH EXCEL.xlsm").Worksheets("Sheet1").Range("A" &
r + 1).VALUE = "TOTAL " & TOTPRIME & " PRIME NUMBERS FOUND
BETWEEN " & N1 & " AND " & N2
Workbooks("PLAY WITH EXCEL.xlsm").Worksheets("Sheet1").Range("A" &
r + 1).Select
Exit Sub
ERR:
MsgBox ERR.Number & " " & ERR.Description
End Sub
```

22

Find Mismatches Between Sheets

Sub Find_Mismatches_Between_Sheets()

```
On Error GoTo ERR
    Dim ic, lc, ir, lr, J, k, hello As Long
    Dim l, M, N As Integer
    M = Sheets.COUNT
    For N = 1 To M
    If Worksheets(N).Name = "Old" Then
    N = 0
    Exit For
    End If
    Next
    If N <> 0 Then
    MsgBox ("For Finding Mismatches/Differences between two Sheets, first you need to copy both Sheets to this Excel file : PLAY WITH EXCEL.XLSM. Then you need to rename both Sheets as Old and New.")
    Exit Sub
    End If
    For N = 1 To M
    If Worksheets(N).Name = "New" Then
    N = 0
    Exit For
    End If
```

```
Next
If N <> 0 Then
MsgBox ("For Finding Mismatches/Differences between two Sheets, first you need to copy both Sheets to this Excel file : PLAY WITH EXCEL.XLSM. Then you need to rename both Sheets as Old and New.")
Exit Sub
End If
ic = Int(InputBox("Enter begining Column No from where you want me to check for Mismatches."))
If ic < 1 Or ic = Empty Then ic = 1
lc = Int(InputBox("Enter Last Column No upto where you want me to check for Mismatches."))
If lc < ic Or lc = Empty Then
hello = lc
lc = ic
ic = hello
End If
ir = Int(InputBox("Enter begining Row No from where you want me to check for Mismatches."))
If ir < 1 Or ir = Empty Then ir = 1
lr = Int(InputBox("Enter Last Row No upto where you want me to check for Mismatches."))
If lr < ir Or lr = Empty Then
hello = lr
lr = ir
ir = hello
End If
l = 5
M = Sheets.COUNT
For N = 1 To M
If Worksheets(N).Name = "LOCATE MISMATCH" Then
N = 0
Exit For
End If
Next
If N > 0 Then
Sheets.Add After:=Sheets(Sheets.COUNT)
Sheets(Sheets.COUNT).Select
```

```
Sheets(Sheets.COUNT).Name = "LOCATE MISMATCH"
End If
Sheets("LOCATE MISMATCH").Range("A1:D50000").VALUE = ""
For J = ir To lr
For k = ic To lc
If Sheets("OLD").Cells(J, k).VALUE <> Sheets("NEW").Cells(J, k).VALUE Then
l = l + 1
Sheets("LOCATE MISMATCH").Range("B" & l).VALUE = Sheets("OLD").Cells(J, k).Address
Sheets("LOCATE MISMATCH").Range("C" & l).VALUE = Sheets("OLD").Cells(J, k).VALUE
Sheets("LOCATE MISMATCH").Range("D" & l).VALUE = Sheets("NEW").Cells(J, k).VALUE
Sheets("LOCATE MISMATCH").Range("B" & l).Select
If Selection.RowHeight > 70 Then Selection.RowHeight = 50
End If
Next
Next
If l > 5 Then
Sheets("LOCATE MISMATCH").Range("B5").VALUE = l - 5 & "MISMATCHES ARE FOUND AT FOLLOWING CELL ADDRESSES:"
Sheets("LOCATE MISMATCH").Range("C5").VALUE = "OLD VALUES:"
Sheets("LOCATE MISMATCH").Range("D5").VALUE = "NEW VALUES:"
Else
Sheets("LOCATE MISMATCH").Range("B5").VALUE = "THERE ARE NO MISMATCHES BETWEEN BOTH SHEETS Old and New."
End If
MsgBox ("Total " & l - 5 & " MISMATHES ARE FOUND!")
Sheets("LOCATE MISMATCH").Select
Columns("B:B").EntireColumn.AutoFit
Columns("C:C").EntireColumn.AutoFit
Columns("D:D").EntireColumn.AutoFit
Sheets("LOCATE MISMATCH").Range("B6").Select
Exit Sub
ERR:
MsgBox ERR.Number & " " & ERR.Description
End Sub
```

23

Show Time

Sub Show_Time()

```
On Error GoTo ERR
    Dim N, N2, N4, SEC1, SEC2 As Integer
    Dim N3 As Long
    N = 0
    N2 = 0
    N3 = 0
    N4 = 0
    SEC1 = 0
    SEC2 = 0
    Workbooks("PLAY WITH EXCEL.xlsm").Worksheets("Sheet1").Activate
    Workbooks("PLAY                                                WITH
EXCEL.xlsm").Worksheets("Sheet1").Range("B2:E3").Select
    With Selection.Font
    .Size = 20
    End With
    Selection.RowHeight = 40
    N2 = Selection.ColumnWidth
    Selection.ColumnWidth = 20
    Workbooks("PLAY                                                WITH
EXCEL.xlsm").Worksheets("Sheet1").Range("B2").VALUE = "HOUR"
    Workbooks("PLAY                                                WITH
EXCEL.xlsm").Worksheets("Sheet1").Range("C2").VALUE = "MINUTES"
```

```
Workbooks("PLAY WITH EXCEL.xlsm").Worksheets("Sheet1").Range("D2").VALUE = "SECONDS"
Workbooks("PLAY WITH EXCEL.xlsm").Worksheets("Sheet1").Range("E2").VALUE = "MILI SEC/10"
Workbooks("PLAY WITH EXCEL.xlsm").Worksheets("Sheet1").Range("E3").VALUE = "Measuring Procesor Speed"
SEC1 = Second(Now())
WILL_COME_BACK:
SEC2 = Second(Now())
If SEC2 < SEC1 Then
SEC2 = (60 - SEC1) + SEC2
Else
SEC2 = SEC2 - SEC1
End If
If SEC2 > 10 Then
Application.Wait (Now + TimeValue("0:00:02"))
Workbooks("PLAY WITH EXCEL.xlsm").Worksheets("Sheet1").Range("B2:E3").VALUE = ""
Workbooks("PLAY WITH EXCEL.xlsm").Worksheets("Sheet1").Range("B2:E3").Select
With Selection.Font
.Size = 11
End With
Selection.ColumnWidth = N2
Workbooks("PLAY WITH EXCEL.xlsm").Worksheets("Sheet1").Range("B2:E3").Select
Selection.RowHeight = 15
Workbooks("PLAY WITH EXCEL.xlsm").Worksheets("Sheet1").Range("A1").Select
Exit Sub
End If
Workbooks("PLAY WITH EXCEL.xlsm").Worksheets("Sheet1").Range("B3").VALUE = Hour(Now())
Workbooks("PLAY WITH EXCEL.xlsm").Worksheets("Sheet1").Range("C3").VALUE = Minute(Now())
Workbooks("PLAY WITH EXCEL.xlsm").Worksheets("Sheet1").Range("D3").VALUE = Second(Now())
```

```
If SEC2 = 2 Then N3 = N3 + 1
If SEC2 > 2 Then
N4 = N4 + 1
If N4 > N3 Then N4 = 0
Workbooks("PLAY WITH EXCEL.xlsm").Worksheets("Sheet1").Range("E3").VALUE = Int(N4 / Int(N3 / 100))
End If
GoTo WILL_COME_BACK
Exit Sub
ERR:
MsgBox ERR.Number & " " & ERR.Description
End Sub
```

24

Rupees in Words

Sub Rupees_in_Words()

```
On Error GoTo ERR
    Dim S1(30), s(11), RS, rs1, SS, PAISA, RUPEE As String
    Workbooks("PLAY WITH EXCEL.xlsm").Worksheets("Sheet1").Activate
    Workbooks("PLAY WITH EXCEL.xlsm").Worksheets("Sheet1").Range("A1").Select
    MsgBox ("This Macro will write Rupees in Words of Cells B2 to B20 in Cells C2 to C20. For blank cells or non numeric data it will add random figures by itself.")
    Workbooks("PLAY WITH EXCEL.xlsm").Worksheets("Sheet1").Range("C2:Z100").VALUE = ""
    Workbooks("PLAY WITH EXCEL.xlsm").Worksheets("Sheet1").Range("A1:Z100").Select
    With Selection.Font
    .Size = 11
    End With
    Workbooks("PLAY WITH EXCEL.xlsm").Worksheets("Sheet1").Range("B2").Select
    PAISA = ""
    RUPEE = ""
    RS = ""
    rs1 = ""
    S1(0) = "One "
    S1(1) = "Two "
```

```
S1(2) = "Three "
S1(3) = "Four "
S1(4) = "Five "
S1(5) = "Six "
S1(6) = "Seven "
S1(7) = "Eight "
S1(8) = "Nine "
S1(9) = "Ten "
S1(10) = "Eleven "
S1(11) = "Twelve "
S1(12) = "Thirteen "
S1(13) = "Fourteen "
S1(14) = "Fifteen "
S1(15) = "Sixteen "
S1(16) = "Seventeen "
S1(17) = "Eighteen "
S1(18) = "Nineteen "
S1(19) = "Twenty "
S1(20) = "Thirty "
S1(21) = "Forty "
S1(22) = "Fifty "
S1(23) = "Sixty "
S1(24) = "Seventy "
S1(25) = "Eighty "
S1(26) = "Ninety "
S1(27) = "Hundred "
S1(28) = "Thousand "
S1(29) = "Lacs "
For J = 2 To 20
SS = Workbooks("PLAY WITH EXCEL.xlsm").Worksheets("Sheet1").Range("B" & J).VALUE
If SS = "" Then SS = Str(Int(1 + Rnd * (10000 - 1 + 1)))
If IsNumeric(SS) = False Then SS = Str(Int(1 + Rnd * (10000 - 1 + 1)))
SS = Trim(SS)
PAISA = ""
RUPEE = ""
RS = ""
rs1 = ""
```

```
Workbooks("PLAY WITH EXCEL.xlsm").Worksheets("Sheet1").Range("B" &
J).VALUE = SS
For I = 1 To Len(SS)
If Mid(SS, I, 1) = "." Or Mid(SS, I, 1) = "." Then
RS = Left(SS, I - 1)
PAISA = Mid(SS, I + 1, 2)
If Len(PAISA) = 1 Then PAISA = PAISA & "0"
I = -10
Exit For
End If
Next
If I <> -10 Then RS = SS
If Right(RS, 1) = "." Or Right(RS, 1) = "." Then RS = Left(RS, Len(RS) - 1)
If Len(RS) > 7 Then
rs1 = Left(RS, Len(RS) - 7)
RS = Right(RS, 7)
End If
If Len(rs1) > 7 Then TRS1 = Right(rs1, 7)
PART2:
If Len(RS) = 7 Then
If Int(Left(RS, 1)) = 1 Then
s(0) = S1(Int(Mid(RS, 2, 1)) + 9)
ElseIf Int(Left(RS, 1)) > 1 Then
s(0) = S1(Int(Left(RS, 1)) + 17)
If Int(Mid(RS, 2, 1)) <> 0 Then s(1) = S1(Int(Mid(RS, 2, 1)) - 1)
Else
If Int(Mid(RS, 2, 1)) <> 0 Then s(1) = S1(Int(Mid(RS, 2, 1)) - 1)
End If
If s(0) <> "" Or s(1) <> "" Then s(2) = S1(29)
End If
If Len(RS) = 6 Then
If Int(Left(RS, 1)) > 0 Then
s(0) = S1(Int(Left(RS, 1)) - 1)
s(1) = S1(29)
End If
End If
If Len(RS) > 4 Then
If Int(Left(Right(RS, 5), 1)) = 1 Then
```

```
s(3) = S1(Int(Left(Right(RS, 4), 1)) + 9)
ElseIf Int(Left(Right(RS, 5), 1)) > 1 Then
s(3) = S1(Left(Right(RS, 5), 1) + 17)
If Int(Left(Right(RS, 4), 1)) <> 0 Then s(4) = S1(Int(Left(Right(RS, 4), 1)) - 1)
Else
If Int(Left(Right(RS, 4), 1)) <> 0 Then s(4) = S1(Int(Left(Right(RS, 4), 1)) - 1)
End If
If s(3) <> "" Or s(4) <> "" Then s(5) = S1(28)
End If
If Len(RS) = 4 Then
If Int(Left(RS, 1)) > 0 Then
s(0) = S1(Int(Left(RS, 1)) - 1)
s(1) = S1(28)
End If
End If
If Len(RS) > 2 Then
If Int(Left(Right(RS, 3), 1)) <> 0 Then
s(6) = S1(Int(Left(Right(RS, 3), 1)) - 1)
s(7) = S1(27)
End If
End If
If Len(RS) > 1 Then
If Int(Left(Right(RS, 2), 1)) = 1 Then
s(8) = S1(Int(Left(Right(RS, 1), 1)) + 9)
ElseIf Int(Left(Right(RS, 2), 1)) > 1 Then
s(8) = S1(Left(Right(RS, 2), 1) + 17)
If Int(Left(Right(RS, 1), 1)) <> 0 Then s(9) = S1(Int(Left(Right(RS, 1), 1)) - 1)
Else
If Int(Left(Right(RS, 1), 1)) <> 0 Then s(9) = S1(Int(Left(Right(RS, 1), 1)) - 1)
End If
End If
If Len(RS) = 1 Then
If Int(Left(RS, 1)) > 0 Then s(0) = S1(Int(Left(RS, 1)) - 1)
End If
RS = ""
RS = s(0) & s(1) & s(2) & s(3) & s(4) & s(5) & s(6) & s(7) & s(8) & s(9)
If Len(PAISA) = 2 Then
If Int(Left(PAISA, 1)) = 1 Then
```

```
s(10) = S1(Int(Mid(PAISA, 2, 1)) + 9)
ElseIf Int(Left(PAISA, 1)) > 1 Then
s(10) = S1(Int(Left(PAISA, 1)) + 17)
If Int(Mid(PAISA, 2, 1)) <> 0 Then s(11) = S1(Int(Mid(PAISA, 2, 1)) - 1)
Else
If Int(Mid(PAISA, 2, 1)) <> 0 Then s(11) = S1(Int(Mid(PAISA, 2, 1)) - 1)
End If
PAISA = ""
If s(10) <> "" Or s(11) <> "" Then PAISA = "And " & s(10) & s(11) & " Paisa "
End If
If RUPEE = "" Then
RUPEE = RS & " " & PAISA
Else
RUPEE = RS & " Crore " & RUPEE
End If
RUPEE = Trim(RUPEE)
Workbooks("PLAY WITH EXCEL.xlsm").Worksheets("Sheet1").Range("C" &
J).VALUE = "INR " & RUPEE & " Only."
PAISA = ""
For I = 0 To 9
s(I) = ""
Next I
RS = rs1
rs1 = ""
If Len(RS) > 0 Then GoTo PART2
Next J
Exit Sub
ERR:
MsgBox ERR.Number & " " & ERR.Description
End Sub
```

25

Merge Cells Separating Data

Sub Merge_Cells_Separating_Data()

```
On Error GoTo ERR
    If ActiveCell.MergeCells = True Then Exit Sub
    Dim CELL As Object
    Dim VAR1 As String
    Dim I As Integer
    MsgBox ("This Macro will merge selected cells without losing data of any cell. If not selected then select cells and Run this Macro again.")
    I = MsgBox("If you have selected cells at more than one places, then all data will be added to one location only. Click No if you don’t want so. Continue?", vbYesNo)
    If I = 7 Then Exit Sub
    VAR1 = ""
    I = 0
    Selection.NumberFormat = "General"
    For Each CELL In Selection
    I = I + 1
    If I > 1 Then VAR1 = VAR1 & “”””
    VAR1 = VAR1 & CELL
    Next CELL
    Selection.ClearContents
    ActiveCell.VALUE = VAR1
    With Selection
    .HorizontalAlignment = xlCenter
```

```
.VerticalAlignment = xlCenter
.WrapText = True
.Orientation = 0
.AddIndent = False
.IndentLevel = 0
.ShrinkToFit = False
.ReadingOrder = xlContext
.MergeCells = False
End With
Selection.Merge
Selection.RowHeight = 15
Selection.ColumnWidth = 8.43
Exit Sub
ERR:
MsgBox ERR.Number & " " & ERR.Description
End Sub
```

26

Unmerge Cells Separating Data

Sub Unmerge_Cells_Separating_Data()

```
On Error GoTo ERR
    MsgBox ("This Macro will unmerge the selected Merged Cell into cells. If not selected then select Merged cell and run this Macro again.")
    If ActiveCell.MergeCells = False Then
    MsgBox ("No Merged Cell Selected!")
    Exit Sub
    End If
    I = MsgBox("You will lose data, if more than one Merged Cell are selected. This Macro works correctly only if one Merged Cell is selected. If selected more that one Merged Cell, then Press NO, otherwise you will lose the data. Continue?", vbYesNo)
    If I = 7 Then Exit Sub
    Dim CELL As Object
    Dim VAR1, var2 As String
    VAR1 = ""
    var2 = ""
    VAR1 = ActiveCell.VALUE
    Selection.NumberFormat = "General"
    Selection.UnMerge
    For Each CELL In Selection
    For I = 1 To Len(VAR1)
    If Mid(VAR1, I, 1) = """" Then
    var2 = Left(VAR1, I - 1)
```

```
VAR1 = Right(VAR1, Len(VAR1) - I)
Exit For
End If
var2 = VAR1
Next I
If var2 <> "" Then CELL = var2
Next CELL
Selection.RowHeight = 15
Selection.ColumnWidth = 8.43
Exit Sub
ERR:
MsgBox ERR.Number & " " & ERR.Description
End Sub
```

27

50 columns 15 rows in One Cell

Sub 50columns_15rows_in_One_Cell()

```
On Error GoTo ERR
    Dim s(15) As Variant
    Workbooks("PLAY WITH EXCEL.xlsm").Worksheets("Sheet1").Activate
    Workbooks("PLAY WITH EXCEL.xlsm").Worksheets("Sheet1").Range("A1").Select
    MsgBox ("Data from cells A1 to AX15 will be added to Cell A16")
    For I = 1 To 15
    For N = 65 To 114
    If N > 90 Then
    s(I - 1) = s(I - 1) & Workbooks("PLAY WITH EXCEL.xlsm").Worksheets("Sheet1").Range("A" & Chr(N - 26) & I).VALUE & "+"
    Else
    s(I - 1) = s(I - 1) & Workbooks("PLAY WITH EXCEL.xlsm").Worksheets("Sheet1").Range(Chr(N) & I).VALUE & "+"
    End If
    Next N
    Next I
    Workbooks("PLAY WITH EXCEL.xlsm").Worksheets("Sheet1").Range("A16").VALUE = ""
    For I = 0 To 14
    Workbooks("PLAY WITH EXCEL.xlsm").Worksheets("Sheet1").Range("A16").VALUE = Workbooks("PLAY WITH EXCEL.xlsm").Worksheets("Sheet1").Range("A16").VALUE & s(I)
```

```
Next I
Workbooks("PLAY WITH EXCEL.xlsm").Worksheets("Sheet1").Range("A16").Select
Exit Sub
ERR:
MsgBox ERR.Number & " " & ERR.Description
End Sub
```

28
Data of Selected Cells in One Cell

Sub Data_of_Selected_Cells_in_One_Cell()

```
On Error GoTo ERR
    Dim S1 As String
    S1 = UCase(InputBox("Enter Column Name & Row number for the result cell - Ex. A15."))
    ActiveSheet.Range(S1).VALUE = ""
    For Each CELL In Selection
    ActiveSheet.Range(S1).VALUE = ActiveSheet.Range(S1).VALUE & CELL & "+"
    Next CELL
    ActiveSheet.Range(S1).Select
    Exit Sub
    ERR:
    MsgBox ERR.Number & " " & ERR.Description
    End Sub
```

29

Encode the Sheet Selected Rows & Cols

Sub Encode_the_Sheet_Selected_Rows_Cols()

```
On Error GoTo ERR
    Dim S1, S2 As Variant
    Dim change(20), CHANGE2(20), l, M As Integer
    Dim ic, lc, ir, lr, hello, J, k As Long
    Workbooks("PLAY WITH EXCEL.xlsm").Worksheets("Sheet1").Activate
    Workbooks("PLAY WITH EXCEL.xlsm").Worksheets("Sheet1").Range("A1").Select
    For I = 1 To 20
    If I < 11 Then
    change(I - 1) = I * I
    CHANGE2(I - 1) = I * 4
    Else
    change(I - 1) = I * 3
    CHANGE2(I - 1) = I * 2
    End If
    Next
    ic = Int(InputBox("Enter begining Column No from where you want to Encode the Data."))
    If ic < 1 Or ic = Empty Then ic = 1
    lc = Int(InputBox("Enter Last Column No upto where you want to Encode the Data."))
```

```
If lc < ic Or lc = Empty Then
hello = lc
lc = ic
ic = hello
End If
ir = Int(InputBox("Enter begining Row No from where you want to Encode the Data."))
If ir < 1 Or ir = Empty Then ir = 1
lr = Int(InputBox("Enter Last Row No upto where you want to Encode the Data."))
If lr < ir Or lr = Empty Then
hello = lr
lr = ir
ir = hello
End If
M = 0
For J = ir To lr
For k = ic To lc
S1 = ""
S1 = """" & Sheets("Sheet1").Cells(J, k).NumberFormat & """"
S1 = S1 & Sheets("Sheet1").Cells(J, k).VALUE
Sheets("Sheet1").Cells(J, k).NumberFormat = "General"
S2 = """"
l = 0
For I = 1 To Len(S1)
S2 = S2 & Chr(Asc(Mid(S1, I, 1)) + change(l) + CHANGE2(M))
l = l + 1
If l > 19 Then l = 0
Next
M = M + 1
If M > 19 Then M = 0
Sheets("Sheet1").Cells(J, k).VALUE = S2
Next
Next
Exit Sub
ERR:
MsgBox ERR.Number & " " & ERR.Description
End Sub
```

30

Decode the Sheet Selected Rows & Cols

Sub Decode_the_Sheet_Selected_Rows_Cols()

```
On Error GoTo ERR
    Dim S1, S2, s3 As Variant
    Dim change(20), CHANGE2(20), l As Integer
    Dim ic, lc, ir, lr, hello, J, k As Long
    Workbooks("PLAY WITH EXCEL.xlsm").Worksheets("Sheet1").Activate
    Workbooks("PLAY WITH
EXCEL.xlsm").Worksheets("Sheet1").Range("A1").Select
    For I = 1 To 20
    If I < 11 Then
    change(I - 1) = I * I
    CHANGE2(I - 1) = I * 4
    Else
    change(I - 1) = I * 3
    CHANGE2(I - 1) = I * 2
    End If
    Next
    MsgBox ("You are required to tell exact Begining and End Columns and
Rows Nos. of Encoded Data.")
    ic = Int(InputBox("Enter begining Column No of the Encoded Data."))
    If ic < 1 Or ic = Empty Then ic = 1
    lc = Int(InputBox("Enter Last Column No of the Encoded Data."))
```

```
If lc < ic Or lc = Empty Then
hello = lc
lc = ic
ic = hello
End If
ir = Int(InputBox("Enter begining Row No of the Encoded Data."))
If ir < 1 Or ir = Empty Then ir = 1
lr = Int(InputBox("Enter Last Row No of the Encoded Data."))
If lr < ir Or lr = Empty Then
hello = lr
lr = ir
ir = hello
End If
M = 0
For J = ir To lr
For k = ic To lc
S1 = ""
S1 = Sheets("Sheet1").Cells(J, k).VALUE
S2 = ""
l = 0
For I = 2 To Len(S1)
S2 = S2 & Chr(Asc(Mid(S1, I, 1)) - (change(l) + CHANGE2(M)))
l = l + 1
If l > 19 Then l = 0
Next
For I = 2 To Len(S2)
If Mid(S2, I, 1) = """" Then
s3 = Mid(S2, 2, I - 2)
S1 = Right(S2, Len(S2) - I)
Exit For
End If
Next
M = M + 1
If M > 19 Then M = 0
If Left(S2, 1) = """" And I <= Len(S2) Then
Sheets("Sheet1").Cells(J, k).VALUE = S1
Sheets("Sheet1").Cells(J, k).Select
Selection.NumberFormat = s3
```

```
End If
Next
Next
Exit Sub
ERR:
MsgBox ERR.Number & " " & ERR.Description
End Sub
```

31

Reverse the Digit Logic 1

Sub Reverse_the_Digit_Logic_1()

```
On Error GoTo ERR
    Dim I, J, REVERSE, MULTIPLYING As Long
    Workbooks("PLAY WITH EXCEL.xlsm").Worksheets("Sheet1").Activate
    Workbooks("PLAY WITH EXCEL.xlsm").Worksheets("Sheet1").Range("A1:Z1000").VALUE = ""
    Workbooks("PLAY WITH EXCEL.xlsm").Worksheets("Sheet1").Range("B2:B3").Select
    Selection.NumberFormat = "General"
    I = 0
    REVERSE = 0
    MULTIPLYING = 1000000000
    I = Int(InputBox("Enter the digit."))
    J = 1
    comeback:
    N = Int(I / J)
    J = J * 10
    N = N Mod 10
    REVERSE = N * MULTIPLYING + REVERSE
    MULTIPLYING = MULTIPLYING / 10
    If J <= I Then GoTo comeback
    REVERSE = REVERSE / (MULTIPLYING * 10)
    Workbooks("PLAY WITH EXCEL.xlsm").Worksheets("Sheet1").Range("B2").VALUE = REVERSE
```

```
Workbooks("PLAY WITH EXCEL.xlsm").Worksheets("Sheet1").Range("B3").VALUE = "Reverse of " & I
Exit Sub
ERR:
MsgBox ERR.Number & " " & ERR.Description
End Sub
```

32

Reverse the Digit Logic 2

Sub Reverse_the_Digit_Logic_2()

```
On Error GoTo ERR
    Dim I, N As Long
    Dim S1, S2 As String
    Workbooks("PLAY WITH EXCEL.xlsm").Worksheets("Sheet1").Activate
    Workbooks("PLAY WITH
EXCEL.xlsm").Worksheets("Sheet1").Range("A1:Z1000").VALUE = ""
    Workbooks("PLAY WITH
EXCEL.xlsm").Worksheets("Sheet1").Range("B2:B3").Select
    Selection.NumberFormat = "General"
    I = 0
    N = 0
    I = Int(InputBox("Enter the digit."))
    S1 = Trim(Str(I))
    For N = Len(S1) To 1 Step -1
    S2 = S2 & Mid(S1, N, 1)
    Next N
    S1 = ""
    For N = 1 To Len(S2)
    If Mid(S2, 1, 1) = "0" Then
    S1 = Right(S2, Len(S2) - N)
    Else
    Exit For
    End If
```

```
Next N
If S1 = "" Then S1 = S2
N = CLng(S1)
Workbooks("PLAY WITH EXCEL.xlsm").Worksheets("Sheet1").Range("B2").VALUE = N
Workbooks("PLAY WITH EXCEL.xlsm").Worksheets("Sheet1").Range("B3").VALUE = "Reverse of " & I
Exit Sub
ERR:
MsgBox ERR.Number & " " & ERR.Description
End Sub
```

33

Reverse the Digit Logic 3

Sub Reverse_the_Digit_Logic_3()

```
On Error GoTo ERR
    Dim I, J, N As Long
    Dim S1, S2 As String
    Workbooks("PLAY WITH EXCEL.xlsm").Worksheets("Sheet1").Activate
    Workbooks("PLAY                                                    WITH
EXCEL.xlsm").Worksheets("Sheet1").Range("A1:Z1000").VALUE = ""
    Workbooks("PLAY                                                    WITH
EXCEL.xlsm").Worksheets("Sheet1").Range("B2:B3").Select
    Selection.NumberFormat = "General"
    I = 0
    S1 = ""
    S2 = ""
    I = Int(InputBox("Enter the digit."))
    J = 1
    comeback:
    N = Int(I / J)
    J = J * 10
    N = N Mod 10
    S1 = S1 & Trim(Str(N))
    If J <= I Then GoTo comeback
    S2 = S1
    S1 = ""
    For N = 1 To Len(S2)
```

```
If Mid(S2, 1, 1) = "0" Then
S1 = Right(S2, Len(S2) - N)
Else
Exit For
End If
Next N
If S1 = "" Then S1 = S2
N = CLng(S1)
Workbooks("PLAY WITH EXCEL.xlsm").Worksheets("Sheet1").Range("B2").VALUE = N
Workbooks("PLAY WITH EXCEL.xlsm").Worksheets("Sheet1").Range("B3").VALUE = "Reverse of " & I
Exit Sub
ERR:
MsgBox ERR.Number & " " & ERR.Description
End Sub
```

34

Sum of Odd Numbers 1 to 100

Sub Sum_of_Odd_Numbers_1to100()

```
On Error GoTo ERR
    Dim SUM, I As Integer
    Workbooks("PLAY WITH EXCEL.xlsm").Worksheets("Sheet1").Activate
    Workbooks("PLAY WITH EXCEL.xlsm").Worksheets("Sheet1").Range("A1:Z1000").VALUE = ""
    Workbooks("PLAY WITH EXCEL.xlsm").Worksheets("Sheet1").Range("B2").Select
    Selection.NumberFormat = "General"
    SUM = 0
    I = 0
    For I = 1 To 99 Step 2
    SUM = SUM + I
    Next I
    Workbooks("PLAY WITH EXCEL.xlsm").Worksheets("Sheet1").Range("B2").VALUE = SUM
    Workbooks("PLAY WITH EXCEL.xlsm").Worksheets("Sheet1").Range("C2").VALUE = "Sum of All Odds between 1 to 100"
    Exit Sub
    ERR:
    MsgBox ERR.Number & " " & ERR.Description
    End Sub
```

35

Sum of Even Numbers 1 to 100

Sub Sum_of_Even_Numbers_1to100()

```
On Error GoTo ERR
    Workbooks("PLAY WITH EXCEL.xlsm").Worksheets("Sheet1").Activate
    Workbooks("PLAY WITH EXCEL.xlsm").Worksheets("Sheet1").Range("A1:Z1000").VALUE = ""
    Workbooks("PLAY WITH EXCEL.xlsm").Worksheets("Sheet1").Range("B2").Select
    Selection.NumberFormat = "General"
    Dim SUM, I As Integer
    SUM = 0
    I = 0
    For I = 2 To 100 Step 2
    SUM = SUM + I
    Next I
    Workbooks("PLAY WITH EXCEL.xlsm").Worksheets("Sheet1").Range("B2").VALUE = SUM
    Workbooks("PLAY WITH EXCEL.xlsm").Worksheets("Sheet1").Range("C2").VALUE = "Sum of All Even between 1 to 100"
    Exit Sub
    ERR:
    MsgBox ERR.Number & " " & ERR.Description
    End Sub
```

36

Table of Given Range Way 1

Sub Table_of_Given_Range_Way1()

```
On Error GoTo ERR
    Dim number1, numnber2, I, J As Integer
    Workbooks("PLAY WITH EXCEL.xlsm").Worksheets("Sheet1").Activate
    Workbooks("PLAY WITH EXCEL.xlsm").Worksheets("Sheet1").Range("A1").Select
    I = 0
    J = 0
    number1 = InputBox("Enter Start number ? : ")
    number2 = InputBox("Enter End number ? : ")
    Cells.Select
    Selection.ClearContents
    Selection.UnMerge
    Selection.RowHeight = 15
    Selection.ColumnWidth = 8.43
    Selection.NumberFormat = "General"
    Cells(3, 2).VALUE = "Table of " & number1 & " to " & number2
    Workbooks("PLAY WITH EXCEL.xlsm").Worksheets("Sheet1").Range("B3").Select
    With Selection.Font
    .Size = 20
    End With
    Selection.RowHeight = 22
    For I = number1 To number2
```

```
For J = 1 To 10
Cells(J + 4, I - number1 + 2).VALUE = I * J
Next J
Next I
Exit Sub
ERR:
MsgBox ERR.Number & " " & ERR.Description
End Sub
```

37

Table of Given Range Way 2

Sub Table_of_Given_Range_Way2()

```
On Error GoTo ERR
    Dim number1, numnber2, I, J As Integer
    Workbooks("PLAY WITH EXCEL.xlsm").Worksheets("Sheet1").Activate
    Workbooks("PLAY WITH
EXCEL.xlsm").Worksheets("Sheet1").Range("A1").Select
    I = 0
    J = 0
    number1 = InputBox("Enter Start number ? : ")
    number2 = InputBox("Enter End number ? : ")
    Cells.Select
    Selection.ClearContents
    Selection.UnMerge
    Selection.RowHeight = 15
    Selection.ColumnWidth = 8.43
    Selection.NumberFormat = "General"
    Cells(3, 2).VALUE = "Table of " & number1 & " to " & number2
    Workbooks("PLAY WITH
EXCEL.xlsm").Worksheets("Sheet1").Range("B3").Select
    With Selection.Font
    .Size = 20
    End With
    Selection.RowHeight = 22
    For I = 1 To 10
```

```
For J = number1 To number2
Workbooks("PLAY WITH EXCEL.xlsm").Worksheets("Sheet1").Range(Chr(65 + I) & J - number1 + 5).VALUE = I * J
Next J
Next I
Exit Sub
ERR:
MsgBox ERR.Number & " " & ERR.Description
End Sub
```

38

Product of Selected Cells

Sub Product_of_Selected_Cells()

```
On Error GoTo ERR
    Dim VAR1 As Double
    VAR1 = 1
    Dim CELL As Object
    Selection.NumberFormat = "General"
    For Each CELL In Selection
    If IsNumeric(CELL) = True Then
    If CELL.VALUE <> "" Then VAR1 = VAR1 * CELL
    End If
    Next CELL
    var2 = InputBox("Enter the Cell Address in which you want the result to see.")
    'Workbooks("PLAY WITH EXCEL.xlsm").Worksheets("Sheet1").Activate
    'Workbooks("PLAY WITH EXCEL.xlsm").Worksheets("Sheet1").Range(var2).Select
    Selection.NumberFormat = "0.00"
    'Workbooks("PLAY WITH EXCEL.xlsm").Worksheets("Sheet1").Range(var2).VALUE = VAR1
    ActiveSheet.Range(var2).VALUE = VAR1
    Exit Sub
    ERR:
    If ERR.Number = 6 Then
    MsgBox "Due to data overflow, it can't give the result."
```

```
Else
MsgBox ERR.Number & " " & ERR.Description
End If
End Sub
```

39
Change Case of Selected Cells

Sub Change_Case_Selected_Cells()

```
On Error GoTo ERR
    Dim s, S1 As String
    Dim N As Integer
    N = 0
    s = ""
    S1 = ""
    Dim CELL As Object
    Selection.NumberFormat = "General"
    N = InputBox("Enter 1 for AllCaps, 2 for AllSmall, 3 for Capital Each Word,
4 for for ToggleCase.")
    If N = 1 Then
    For Each CELL In Selection
    s = UCase(CELL)
    CELL.VALUE = s
    Next CELL
    ElseIf N = 2 Then
    For Each CELL In Selection
    s = LCase(CELL)
    CELL.VALUE = s
    Next CELL
    ElseIf N = 3 Then
    For Each CELL In Selection
    s = (CELL)
```

```
S1 = ""
For I = 1 To Len(s)
If Mid(s, I, 1) = " " Then
I = I + 1
If I <= Len(s) Then
S1 = S1 & " " & UCase(Mid(s, I, 1))
Else
S1 = S1 & " "
End If
Else
S1 = S1 & LCase(Mid(s, I, 1))
End If
Next I
s = UCase(Left(S1, 1)) & Right(S1, Len(S1) - 1)
CELL.VALUE = s
Next CELL
ElseIf N = 4 Then
For Each CELL In Selection
s = (CELL)
S1 = ""
For I = 1 To Len(s)
If Asc(Mid(s, I, 1)) > 64 And Asc(Mid(s, I, 1)) < 91 Then
S1 = S1 & Chr(Asc(Mid(s, I, 1)) + 32)
ElseIf Asc(Mid(s, I, 1)) > 96 And Asc(Mid(s, I, 1)) < 123 Then
S1 = S1 & Chr(Asc(Mid(s, I, 1)) - 32)
Else
S1 = S1 & Mid(s, I, 1)
End If
Next I
CELL.VALUE = S1
Next CELL
Else
MsgBox ("No Proper Instruction Feeded.")
End If
Exit Sub
ERR:
MsgBox ERR.Number & " " & ERR.Description
End Sub
```

40

Trim Selected Cells

Sub Trim_Selected_Cells()

```
On Error GoTo ERR
    Dim s, S1 As String
    s = ""
    S1 = ""
    Dim CELL As Object
    Selection.NumberFormat = "General"
    For Each CELL In Selection
    s = CELL
    s = Trim(s)
    S1 = ""
    For I = 1 To Len(s)
    If Mid(s, I, 1) = " " Then
    If Len(S1) >= 0 Then
    If Right(S1, 1) <> " " Then S1 = S1 & " "
    Else
    S1 = S1 & " "
    End If
    Else
    S1 = S1 & Mid(s, I, 1)
    End If
    Next I
    CELL.VALUE = S1
    Next CELL
```

```
Exit Sub
ERR:
MsgBox ERR.Number & " " & ERR.Description
End Sub
```

41

Shift Data in Reverse Order

Sub Shift_Data_in_Reverse_Order()

```
On Error GoTo ERR
    Dim s(1000) As Variant
    Dim N As Integer
    Dim CELL As Object
    Selection.NumberFormat = "General"
    N = 0
    For Each CELL In Selection
    s(N) = CELL
    N = N + 1
    Next CELL
    N = N - 1
    For Each CELL In Selection
    CELL = s(N)
    N = N - 1
    Next CELL
    Exit Sub
    ERR:
    MsgBox ERR.Number & " " & ERR.Description
    End Sub
```

42

Animate the Sheet Ex One

Sub Animate_the_Sheet_Ex_One()

```
On Error GoTo ERR
    Dim N As Long
    Workbooks("PLAY WITH EXCEL.xlsm").Worksheets("Sheet1").Activate
    Workbooks("PLAY WITH EXCEL.xlsm").Worksheets("Sheet1").Range("A1").Select
    N = InputBox("ENTER NUMBER BETWEEN 1 TO 10 TO CONTROL THE SPEED: 1 = TOP SPEED, 10 = LEAST SPEED.")
    If IsNumeric(N) = False Then N = 1
    If N > 0 And N < 11 Then
    N = N * 100000
    Else
    N = 1
    End If
    For J = 66 To 76
    For I = 2 To 18
    Workbooks("PLAY WITH EXCEL.xlsm").Worksheets("Sheet1").Range(Chr(J) & I).Select
    For k = 1 To N
    Next k
    Next I
    For I = 18 To 2 Step -1
    Workbooks("PLAY WITH EXCEL.xlsm").Worksheets("Sheet1").Range(Chr(J) & I).Select
```

```
For k = 1 To N
Next k
Next I
Next J
For J = 76 To 66 Step -1
For I = 2 To 18
Workbooks("PLAY WITH EXCEL.xlsm").Worksheets("Sheet1").Range(Chr(J) & I).Select
For k = 1 To N
Next k
Next I
For I = 18 To 2 Step -1
Workbooks("PLAY WITH EXCEL.xlsm").Worksheets("Sheet1").Range(Chr(J) & I).Select
For k = 1 To N
Next k
Next I
Next J
Exit Sub
ERR:
MsgBox ERR.Number & " " & ERR.Description
End Sub
```

43

Animate the Sheet Ex Two

Sub Animate_the_Sheet_ Ex_Two()

```
On Error GoTo ERR
    Dim N As Long
    Workbooks("PLAY WITH EXCEL.xlsm").Worksheets("Sheet1").Activate
    Workbooks("PLAY WITH EXCEL.xlsm").Worksheets("Sheet1").Range("A1").Select
    N = InputBox("ENTER NUMBER BETWEEN 1 TO 10 TO CONTROL THE SPEED: 1 = TOP SPEED, 10 = LEAST SPEED.")
    If IsNumeric(N) = False Then N = 1
    If N > 0 And N < 11 Then
    N = N * 100000
    Else
    N = 1
    End If
    For J = 65 To 80
    For I = 2 To 20
    Workbooks("PLAY WITH EXCEL.xlsm").Worksheets("Sheet1").Range(Chr(J) & I).Select
    For k = 1 To N
    Next k
    Next I
    Next J
    For J = 80 To 65 Step -1
    For I = 2 To 20
```

```
Workbooks("PLAY WITH EXCEL.xlsm").Worksheets("Sheet1").Range(Chr(J) & I).Select
For k = 1 To N
Next k
Next I
Next J
Exit Sub
ERR:
MsgBox ERR.Number & " " & ERR.Description
End Sub
```

44

Animate the Sheet Ex Three

Sub Animate_the_Sheet_Ex_Three()

```
On Error GoTo ERR
    Dim N As Long
    Dim N1, N2, N3, N4 As Integer
    Workbooks("PLAY WITH EXCEL.xlsm").Worksheets("Sheet1").Activate
    Workbooks("PLAY WITH EXCEL.xlsm").Worksheets("Sheet1").Range("A1").Select
    N1 = 65
    N2 = 76
    N3 = 2
    N4 = 18
    N = InputBox("ENTER NUMBER BETWEEN 1 TO 10 TO CONTROL THE SPEED: 1 = TOP SPEED, 10 = LEAST SPEED.")
    If IsNumeric(N) = False Then N = 1
    If N > 0 And N < 11 Then
    N = N * 100000
    Else
    N = 1
    End If
    For I = 1 To 5
    For J = N1 To N2
    Workbooks("PLAY WITH EXCEL.xlsm").Worksheets("Sheet1").Range(Chr(J) & N3).Select
    With Selection.Interior
```

```
.Pattern = xlSolid
.PatternColorIndex = xlAutomatic
.Color = 15773696
.TintAndShade = 0
.PatternTintAndShade = 0
End With
For k = 1 To N
Next k
Next J
For J = N3 To N4
Workbooks("PLAY WITH
EXCEL.xlsm").Worksheets("Sheet1").Range(Chr(N2) & J).Select
With Selection.Interior
.Pattern = xlSolid
.PatternColorIndex = xlAutomatic
.Color = 15773696
.TintAndShade = 0
.PatternTintAndShade = 0
End With
For k = 1 To N
Next k
Next J
For J = N2 To N1 Step -1
Workbooks("PLAY WITH
EXCEL.xlsm").Worksheets("Sheet1").Range(Chr(J) & N4).Select
With Selection.Interior
.Pattern = xlSolid
.PatternColorIndex = xlAutomatic
.Color = 15773696
.TintAndShade = 0
.PatternTintAndShade = 0
End With
For k = 1 To N
Next k
Next J
N3 = N3 + 1
For J = N4 To N3 Step -1
```

```
Workbooks("PLAY WITH
EXCEL.xlsm").Worksheets("Sheet1").Range(Chr(N1) & J).Select
With Selection.Interior
.Pattern = xlSolid
.PatternColorIndex = xlAutomatic
.Color = 15773696
.TintAndShade = 0
.PatternTintAndShade = 0
End With
For k = 1 To N
Next k
Next J
N1 = N1 + 1
N2 = N2 - 1
N4 = N4 - 1
Next I
Workbooks("PLAY WITH
EXCEL.xlsm").Worksheets("Sheet1").Range("A2:L18").Select
With Selection.Interior
.Pattern = xlNone
.TintAndShade = 0
.PatternTintAndShade = 0
End With
Workbooks("PLAY WITH
EXCEL.xlsm").Worksheets("Sheet1").Range("A1").Select
Exit Sub
ERR:
MsgBox ERR.Number & " " & ERR.Description
End Sub
```

45

Animate the Sheet Ex Four

Sub Animate_the_Sheet_Ex_Four()

```
On Error GoTo ERR
    Workbooks("PLAY WITH EXCEL.xlsm").Worksheets("Sheet1").Activate
    Workbooks("PLAY WITH EXCEL.xlsm").Worksheets("Sheet1").Range("B2").Select
    For J = 1 To 5
    For I = 1 To 100
    Selection.ColumnWidth = Selection.ColumnWidth + 1
    Next I
    For I = 1 To 100
    Selection.ColumnWidth = Selection.ColumnWidth - 1
    Next I
    For I = 1 To 100
    Selection.RowHeight = Selection.RowHeight + 2
    Next I
    For I = 1 To 100
    Selection.RowHeight = Selection.RowHeight - 2
    Next I
    For I = 1 To 100
    Selection.RowHeight = Selection.RowHeight + 2
    Selection.ColumnWidth = Selection.ColumnWidth + 1
    Next I
    For I = 1 To 100
    Selection.RowHeight = Selection.RowHeight - 2
```

```
Selection.ColumnWidth = Selection.ColumnWidth - 1
Next I
Next J
Exit Sub
ERR:
MsgBox ERR.Number & " " & ERR.Description
End Sub
```

46

Animate the Sheet Ex Five

Sub Animate_the_Sheet_Ex_Five()

```
On Error GoTo ERR
    Dim N1, N2, N3 As Integer
    Workbooks("PLAY WITH EXCEL.xlsm").Worksheets("Sheet1").Activate
    Workbooks("PLAY WITH EXCEL.xlsm").Worksheets("Sheet1").Range("A1").Select
    For J = 1 To 4
    For I = 1 To 400
    N1 = Int(65 + Rnd * (76 - 65 + 1))
    N2 = Int(1 + Rnd * (20 - 1 + 1))
    N3 = Int(100 + Rnd * (1000 - 100 + 1))
    Workbooks("PLAY WITH EXCEL.xlsm").Worksheets("Sheet1").Range(Chr(N1) & N2).Select
    With Selection.Interior
    .Pattern = xlSolid
    .PatternColorIndex = xlAutomatic
    .Color = N1 * N2 * N3
    .TintAndShade = 0
    .PatternTintAndShade = 0
    End With
    Next I
    Workbooks("PLAY WITH EXCEL.xlsm").Worksheets("Sheet1").Range("A1:L20").Select
    With Selection.Interior
```

```
.Pattern = xlNone
.TintAndShade = 0
.PatternTintAndShade = 0
End With
Workbooks("PLAY WITH EXCEL.xlsm").Worksheets("Sheet1").Range("A1").Select
Next J
Exit Sub
ERR:
MsgBox ERR.Number & " " & ERR.Description
End Sub
```

47

Animate the Sheet Ex Six

Sub Animate_the_Sheet_Ex_Six()

```
On Error GoTo ERR
    Dim s As String
    Workbooks("PLAY WITH EXCEL.xlsm").Worksheets("Sheet1").Activate
    Workbooks("PLAY WITH EXCEL.xlsm").Worksheets("Sheet1").Range("A1").Select
    s = "PRESENTING DIFFERENT CHARTS WITH DEMO DATA ---- "
    Workbooks("PLAY WITH EXCEL.xlsm").Worksheets("Sheet1").Range("A1:Z100").VALUE = ""
    Workbooks("PLAY WITH EXCEL.xlsm").Worksheets("Sheet1").Range("A1:Z100").Select
    Selection.RowHeight = 20
    Workbooks("PLAY WITH EXCEL.xlsm").Worksheets("Sheet1").Range("A17").VALUE = s
    Workbooks("PLAY WITH EXCEL.xlsm").Worksheets("Sheet1").Range("A17").Select
    With Selection.Font
    .Size = 18
    End With
    Application.Wait (Now + TimeValue("0:00:01"))
    Workbooks("PLAY WITH EXCEL.xlsm").Worksheets("Sheet1").Range("B2").VALUE = "INCOME/MONTH"
```

```
Workbooks("PLAY WITH EXCEL.xlsm").Worksheets("Sheet1").Range("B3").VALUE = "RAM"
Workbooks("PLAY WITH EXCEL.xlsm").Worksheets("Sheet1").Range("B4").VALUE = "MOHAN"
Workbooks("PLAY WITH EXCEL.xlsm").Worksheets("Sheet1").Range("B5").VALUE = "SOHAN"
Workbooks("PLAY WITH EXCEL.xlsm").Worksheets("Sheet1").Range("B6").VALUE = "SHANKAR"
Application.Wait (Now + TimeValue("0:00:01"))
Workbooks("PLAY WITH EXCEL.xlsm").Worksheets("Sheet1").Range("C2").VALUE = "JAN-20"
Workbooks("PLAY WITH EXCEL.xlsm").Worksheets("Sheet1").Range("C3").VALUE = "40000"
Workbooks("PLAY WITH EXCEL.xlsm").Worksheets("Sheet1").Range("C4").VALUE = "45000"
Workbooks("PLAY WITH EXCEL.xlsm").Worksheets("Sheet1").Range("C5").VALUE = "50000"
Workbooks("PLAY WITH EXCEL.xlsm").Worksheets("Sheet1").Range("C6").VALUE = "35000"
Application.Wait (Now + TimeValue("0:00:01"))
Workbooks("PLAY WITH EXCEL.xlsm").Worksheets("Sheet1").Range("D2").VALUE = "FEB-20"
Workbooks("PLAY WITH EXCEL.xlsm").Worksheets("Sheet1").Range("D3").VALUE = "30000"
Workbooks("PLAY WITH EXCEL.xlsm").Worksheets("Sheet1").Range("D4").VALUE = "25000"
Workbooks("PLAY WITH EXCEL.xlsm").Worksheets("Sheet1").Range("D5").VALUE = "20000"
Workbooks("PLAY WITH EXCEL.xlsm").Worksheets("Sheet1").Range("D6").VALUE = "55000"
Application.Wait (Now + TimeValue("0:00:01"))
Workbooks("PLAY WITH EXCEL.xlsm").Worksheets("Sheet1").Range("E2").VALUE = "MAR-20"
Workbooks("PLAY WITH EXCEL.xlsm").Worksheets("Sheet1").Range("E3").VALUE = "33000"
Workbooks("PLAY WITH EXCEL.xlsm").Worksheets("Sheet1").Range("E4").VALUE = "15000"
```

```
    Workbooks("PLAY WITH EXCEL.xlsm").Worksheets("Sheet1").Range("E5").VALUE = "10000"
    Workbooks("PLAY WITH EXCEL.xlsm").Worksheets("Sheet1").Range("E6").VALUE = "10000"
    Application.Wait (Now + TimeValue("0:00:01"))
    Workbooks("PLAY WITH EXCEL.xlsm").Worksheets("Sheet1").Range("F2").VALUE = "APR-20"
    Workbooks("PLAY WITH EXCEL.xlsm").Worksheets("Sheet1").Range("F3").VALUE = "50000"
    Workbooks("PLAY WITH EXCEL.xlsm").Worksheets("Sheet1").Range("F4").VALUE = "65000"
    Workbooks("PLAY WITH EXCEL.xlsm").Worksheets("Sheet1").Range("F5").VALUE = "40000"
    Workbooks("PLAY WITH EXCEL.xlsm").Worksheets("Sheet1").Range("F6").VALUE = "70000"
    Application.Wait (Now + TimeValue("0:00:01"))
    s = s & "CHART TYPE : "
    Workbooks("PLAY WITH EXCEL.xlsm").Worksheets("Sheet1").Range("B2:F6").Select
    Workbooks("PLAY WITH EXCEL.xlsm").Worksheets("Sheet1").Shapes.AddChart.Select
    ActiveChart.SetSourceData Source:=Range("Sheet1!$B$2:$F$6")
    ActiveChart.ChartType = xlColumnClustered
    Application.Wait (Now + TimeValue("0:00:01"))
    Workbooks("PLAY WITH EXCEL.xlsm").Worksheets("Sheet1").Range("A17").VALUE = s & "xlColumnClustered"
    ActiveChart.ChartType = xlColumnStacked
    Application.Wait (Now + TimeValue("0:00:02"))
    Workbooks("PLAY WITH EXCEL.xlsm").Worksheets("Sheet1").Range("A17").VALUE = s & "xlColumnStacked"
    ActiveChart.ChartType = xlCylinderColClustered
    Application.Wait (Now + TimeValue("0:00:02"))
    Workbooks("PLAY WITH EXCEL.xlsm").Worksheets("Sheet1").Range("A17").VALUE = s & "xlCylinderColClustered"
    ActiveChart.ChartType = xlLine
```

```
    Application.Wait (Now + TimeValue("0:00:02"))
    Workbooks("PLAY WITH EXCEL.xlsm").Worksheets("Sheet1").Range("A17").VALUE = s & "xlLine"
    ActiveChart.ChartType = xl3DLine
    Application.Wait (Now + TimeValue("0:00:02"))
    Workbooks("PLAY WITH EXCEL.xlsm").Worksheets("Sheet1").Range("A17").VALUE = s & "xl3DLine"
    ActiveChart.ChartType = xlPie
    Application.Wait (Now + TimeValue("0:00:02"))
    Workbooks("PLAY WITH EXCEL.xlsm").Worksheets("Sheet1").Range("A17").VALUE = s & "xlPie"
    ActiveChart.ChartType = xl3DPie
    Application.Wait (Now + TimeValue("0:00:02"))
    Workbooks("PLAY WITH EXCEL.xlsm").Worksheets("Sheet1").Range("A17").VALUE = s & "xl3DPie"
    ActiveChart.ChartType = xlBarOfPie
    Application.Wait (Now + TimeValue("0:00:02"))
    Workbooks("PLAY WITH EXCEL.xlsm").Worksheets("Sheet1").Range("A17").VALUE = s & "xlBarOfPie"
    ActiveChart.ChartType = xlBarClustered
    Application.Wait (Now + TimeValue("0:00:02"))
    Workbooks("PLAY WITH EXCEL.xlsm").Worksheets("Sheet1").Range("A17").VALUE = s & "xlBarClustered"
    ActiveChart.ChartType = xlArea
    Application.Wait (Now + TimeValue("0:00:02"))
    Workbooks("PLAY WITH EXCEL.xlsm").Worksheets("Sheet1").Range("A17").VALUE = s & "xlArea"
    ActiveChart.ChartType = xlXYScatter
    Application.Wait (Now + TimeValue("0:00:02"))
    Workbooks("PLAY WITH EXCEL.xlsm").Worksheets("Sheet1").Range("A17").VALUE = s & "xlXYScatter"
    ActiveChart.ChartType = xlXYScatterSmooth
    Application.Wait (Now + TimeValue("0:00:02"))
    Workbooks("PLAY WITH EXCEL.xlsm").Worksheets("Sheet1").Range("A17").VALUE = s & "xlXYScatterSmooth"
    ActiveChart.ChartType = xlDoughnut
```

```
Application.Wait (Now + TimeValue("0:00:02"))
Workbooks("PLAY WITH EXCEL.xlsm").Worksheets("Sheet1").Range("A17").VALUE = s & "xlDoughnut"
ActiveChart.ChartType = xlRadar
Application.Wait (Now + TimeValue("0:00:02"))
Workbooks("PLAY WITH EXCEL.xlsm").Worksheets("Sheet1").Range("A17").VALUE = s & "xlRadar"
Application.Wait (Now + TimeValue("0:00:02"))
ActiveChart.Parent.Delete
Workbooks("PLAY WITH EXCEL.xlsm").Worksheets("Sheet1").Range("A1:Z100").VALUE = ""
Workbooks("PLAY WITH EXCEL.xlsm").Worksheets("Sheet1").Range("A17").Select
With Selection.Font
.Size = 11
End With
Workbooks("PLAY WITH EXCEL.xlsm").Worksheets("Sheet1").Range("A1").Select
Exit Sub
ERR:
MsgBox ERR.Number & " " & ERR.Description
End Sub
```

48

Animate the Sheet Ex Seven

Sub Animate_the_Sheet_Ex_Seven()

```
On Error GoTo ERR
    Dim N1, N2 As Integer
    Application.WindowState = xlMaximized
    N1 = Application.Width
    N2 = Application.Height
    Application.WindowState = xlNormal
    Application.Width = N1
    Application.Height = N2
    Application.Left = 0
    Application.Top = 0
    For I = 1 To 70
    Application.Left = Application.Left + 1.5
    Application.Width = Application.Width - 1.5
    Application.Width = Application.Width - 1.5
    Application.Top = Application.Top + 4
    Application.Height = Application.Height - 3
    Application.Height = Application.Height - 3
    Next I
    For I = 1 To 70
    Application.Left = Application.Left - 1.5
    Application.Width = Application.Width + 1.5
    Application.Width = Application.Width + 1.5
    Application.Top = Application.Top - 1.5
```

```
Application.Height = Application.Height + 3
Application.Height = Application.Height + 3
Next I
Application.WindowState = xlMaximized
Exit Sub
ERR:
MsgBox ERR.Number & " " & ERR.Description
End Sub
```

49

Animate the Sheet Ex Eight

Sub Animate_the_Sheet_Ex_Eight()

```
On Error GoTo ERR
    Dim N1, N2 As Integer
    Application.WindowState = xlMaximized
    N1 = Application.Width
    N2 = Application.Height
    Application.WindowState = xlNormal
    Application.Width = N1
    Application.Height = N2
    Application.Left = 0
    Application.Top = 0
    For I = 1 To 375
    Application.Left = Application.Left + 1.5
    Application.Width = Application.Width - 1.5
    Next I
    For I = 1 To 375
    Application.Left = Application.Left - 1.5
    Application.Width = Application.Width + 1.5
    Next I
    Application.WindowState = xlMaximized
    N1 = Application.Width
    N2 = Application.Height
    Application.WindowState = xlNormal
    Application.Width = N1
```

```
Application.Height = N2
Application.Left = 0
Application.Top = 0
For I = 1 To 150
Application.Top = Application.Top + 4
Application.Height = Application.Height - 3
Next I
For I = 1 To 150
Application.Top = Application.Top - 1.5
Application.Height = Application.Height + 3
Next I
Application.WindowState = xlMaximized
Exit Sub
ERR:
MsgBox ERR.Number & " " & ERR.Description
End Sub
```

50

Animate the Sheet Ex Nine

Sub Animate_the_Sheet_Ex_Nine()

```
On Error GoTo ERR
    Workbooks("PLAY WITH EXCEL.xlsm").Worksheets("Sheet1").Activate
    Workbooks("PLAY                                                    WITH
EXCEL.xlsm").Worksheets("Sheet1").Range("A1").Select
    For I = 100 To 10 Step -2
    ActiveWindow.Zoom = I
    Next I
    For I = 10 To 400 Step 2
    ActiveWindow.Zoom = I
    Next I
    For I = 400 To 100 Step -2
    ActiveWindow.Zoom = I
    Next I
    Exit Sub
    ERR:
    MsgBox ERR.Number & " " & ERR.Description
    End Sub
```

51

Animate the Sheet Ex Ten

Sub Animate_the_Sheet_Ex_Ten()

```
On Error GoTo ERR
    Dim N1, N2 As Integer
    N1 = 0
    N2 = 0
    For I = 1 To 5
    N1 = Int(2 + Rnd * (12 - 2 + 1))
    N2 = Int(2 + Rnd * (15 - 2 + 1))
    With ActiveWindow
    .SplitColumn = N1
    .SplitRow = N2
    End With
    Application.Wait (Now + TimeValue("0:00:01"))
    Next I
    For I = 1 To 3
    N1 = Int(2 + Rnd * (12 - 2 + 1))
    N2 = Int(2 + Rnd * (15 - 2 + 1))
    With ActiveWindow
    .SplitColumn = N1
    .SplitRow = N2
    End With
    Application.Wait (Now + TimeValue("0:00:01"))
    Application.DisplayFormulaBar = False
    Application.Wait (Now + TimeValue("0:00:01"))
```

```
ActiveWindow.DisplayHeadings = False
Application.Wait (Now + TimeValue("0:00:01"))
ActiveWindow.DisplayGridlines = False
Application.Wait (Now + TimeValue("0:00:01"))
Application.DisplayFormulaBar = True
Application.Wait (Now + TimeValue("0:00:01"))
ActiveWindow.DisplayHeadings = True
Application.Wait (Now + TimeValue("0:00:01"))
ActiveWindow.DisplayGridlines = True
Application.Wait (Now + TimeValue("0:00:01"))
Next I
With ActiveWindow
.SplitColumn = 0
.SplitRow = 0
End With
ActiveWindow.Zoom = True
ActiveWindow.Zoom = 100
Workbooks("PLAY WITH EXCEL.xlsm").Worksheets("Sheet1").Activate
Workbooks("PLAY WITH EXCEL.xlsm").Worksheets("Sheet1").Range("A1").Select
Exit Sub
ERR:
MsgBox ERR.Number & " " & ERR.Description
End Sub
```

Thanks For Reading...

For suggestions or request for help related to Excel Data Manipulation or VBA, please write to me at below Email Ids:

Email:anurag_k_p@yahoo.co.in

Email: anuragspandey@gmail.com

Face book Profile: https://www.facebook.com/anurag.pandey.98031

Face book Page: https://www.facebook.com/HalfCoockedThoughts/?ref=bookmarks

Twitter: https://twitter.com/ANURAGP64628371

ANURAG S PANDEY

Bhubaneshwar, India

www.ingramcontent.com/pod-product-compliance
Ingram Content Group UK Ltd.
Pitfield, Milton Keynes, MK11 3LW, UK
UKHW041638190726
13854UKWH00006B/2574

9 798889 867814